Praise for *The S*

"Any loss is difficult. Sudden loss can be doubly so. That is why this book is so vital. As the title tells us, this is a survival guide. At a time when you think you can't go on, this remarkable book will show you how you can and why you must. And, it does so in a very easy-to-get, gentle, comforting, and heartfelt way. Exactly what you need at this overwhelming time."

—Allen Klein, author of *Embracing Life After Loss*

"When you have a loss that changes everything, this handbook serves as a gentle, steadfast companion on your most difficult days to guide you from pain and suffering to living again with new, profound meaning. Filled with effective and practical coping strategies, *The Sudden Loss Survival Guide* provides a path to healing for anyone navigating the unfamiliar grounds of sudden loss.

"Using Chelsea Hanson's Seven Essential Grief Healing Practices—a process to transform, heal, and transcend grief— you are led from brokenness to wholeness to not only survive grief, but also grow and evolve over time. This easy-to-read, how-to-heal guide will not only soothe your spirit, but also give you a life-affirming plan to rebuild your shattered world. From her hard-earned wisdom of losing her parents and as a counselor to many grievers, Hanson knows the art of healing and leads you there in this must-read book. You'll learn to not be defined by your loss, but by your continuing love for the person who died."

—Tom Stone, founder and chairman of Inner Greatness Global and author of *Pure Awareness, The Power of How, Vaporize Your Anxiety,* and *Emotional Mastery*

"As a grief counselor, I am a firm believer in learning about what is normal in grief, so we can know what reactions we might expect and what we can do to manage them more effectively in ways that foster healing and growth. This Survival Guide is a treasure trove of useful tools, practical suggestions, and helpful practices which, bundled together in an immensely readable format, will serve as a reliable road map to living through and finding meaning in significant loss."

—Marty Tousley, RN, MS, FT, author of *Finding Your Way through Grief: A Guide for the First Year*

"In this beautiful book of love and light, Chelsea Hanson offers the practice of reconnecting with a loved one in the spiritual realm to continue the relationship in a new, different way. This essential aspect to healing is often missing in traditional grief support books, and Hanson teaches it in a way that anyone can understand and apply. You'll be inspired to believe that you can connect to the spirit of your beloved and use the eternal, unbreakable bond of love to heal."

—Reverend Maggie Chula, author of *Open the Doorway to Your Soul*

"Chelsea's losses have transformed her into a courageous, compassionate teacher for all of us. Wisdom and encouragement jump from the pages to inspire hope and healing. This book is an essential guide for navigating the difficult journey of grief."

—Todd Nigro, founder of Ellie's Way

"Grief is a universal experience. Sooner or later, we all experience grief. When it's triggered by an unexpected loss, it's doubly difficult to handle. Chelsea Hanson's new book, *The Sudden Loss Survival Guide*, is the perfect resource for anyone suddenly confronted with the loss of a loved one. Read it and weep…tears of love and healing."

—BJ Gallagher, coauthor of *Your Life Is Your Prayer*

"Clear, light, and instructive, *The Sudden Loss Survival Guide* empowers us to take small steps on the path from grief and loss to compassionate acceptance. With gentle and loving wisdom, Chelsea Hanson's inward nurturance of her own grieving heart reminds us of our capacity to experience sorrow yet continue our connection to love and light. An intuitive guide of perseverance, renewal, and ultimately growth."

—Bridgitte Jackson-Buckley, author of *The Gift of Crisis*

"A wonderful resource that provides many useful tools! Chelsea Hanson has created a heart-centered guide to working through the many aspects of grief. The exercises are engaging and will touch your soul, helping you to release your grief…one layer at a time. Take the time to read each chapter and allow it to speak to your heart and allow it to help you heal."

—Lori Pederson, founder of *I Did Not Know What to Say*

"*The Sudden Loss Survival Guide* is a must-read guidebook for everyone who has experienced an unexpected loss of any kind in their life. Chelsea Hanson introduces her readers to the 'Seven Rs'—an innovative and in-depth process for healing grief. Chelsea's simple-to-read approach helps anyone experiencing the 'grief brain' better navigate the immediate aftermath of unexpected loss. There are a variety of loss-related topics (e.g. understanding sorrow, letting go, fostering a support system, discovering purpose after loss, and many more) as well as healing concepts, actionable exercises, and reflections that are perfect for someone who has experienced an unexpected loss of any kind. Chelsea becomes the reader's personal cheerleader, lifting and supporting them during one of their most difficult times. This book is a wonderful reminder that grief is not insurmountable, and with courage and action you can move through it in one piece."

—Sharon Ehlers, Advanced Grief Recovery Specialist and author of *Grief Reiki*

The
Sudden
LOSS
Survival Guide

The
Sudden
LOSS
Survival Guide

7 Essential Practices
for Healing Grief

Chelsea Hanson

Coral Gables

Cover Design: Roberto Nuñez
illustration: Adobe stock/ MicroOne
Layout & Design: Liz Hong

For permission requests, please contact the publisher at:
Mango Publishing Group
2850 S Douglas Road, 2nd Floor
Coral Gables, FL 33134 USA
info@mango.bz

For special orders, quantity sales, course adoptions and corporate
sales, please email the publisher at sales@mango.bz. For trade and
wholesale sales, please contact Ingram Publisher Services at customer.
service@ingramcontent.com or +1.800.509.4887.

The Sudden Loss Survivial Guide: 7 Essential Practices
for Healing Grief

Library of Congress Cataloging-in-Publication number: 2020933490
ISBN: (p) 978-1-64250-228-2 (e) 978-1-64250-229-9
BISAC category code FAM014000, FAMILY & RELATIONSHIPS /
Death, Grief, Bereavement

Printed in the United States of America

In honor of my parents

Donna Olson (1935–1996)
Ken Olson (1931–1972)

And dedicated to you, the sudden loss survivor

We don't look to the heavens
to see what we have lost
but to remember those
who have found peace.

Table of Contents

Foreword

Loss and grief catch us by surprise, even when we know that, at some point, we will know them and need a plan to guide us through and beyond their hold. *The Sudden Loss Survival Guide* is one of those indispensable guides for the journey.

When my husband died, I didn't expect to feel totally annihilated, as if blown into scattered, irretrievable bits. Because he was older, I understood the possibility I would outlive him. But I mistakenly believed his death would merely bring great sadness because of how much I'd miss him. At first, I thought he would come back to me, so I went to sleep with my hand extended in the air waiting for him to pull me toward him. When I woke up morning after morning to find myself still here, I thought I should go to him. I researched suicide but couldn't bear the thought of causing pain for those I love. I decided to live instead. Then came the hard part. How to create and live a life without him.

I was guided by a metaphor—the image of beautiful mosaics, formed by broken bits, much like my own life felt at the time. The question became how to put these broken bits together again and what was available to guide me. Chelsea Hanson's *The Sudden Loss Survival Guide* is one such guide. As I began reading the book you are about to begin, I could feel Chelsea holding me and allowing a space for my grief.

There is no guesswork in *The Sudden Loss Survival Guide*. Chelsea clearly states this is a book of transformation and healing. And it doesn't stop there. You're offered practical tools for healing sorrow while not turning away from the raw pain of grief and the profoundness of your loss. And you're guided gently, yet steadily, through a path of healing.

Chelsea knows deep grief too, the kind you may be experiencing. She generously shares her experiences alongside examples of others who've been guided through her process for healing too. Her story includes losing her father at a very early age, and then, when Chelsea was twenty-eight years old, her mother died suddenly at Christmas. Later, she suffered the loss of two unborn children through miscarriage. As you read about her experiences and those of others, you'll begin to see yourself in them. You may realize your unbearable loss is unique, but also shares commonalities with others. Chelsea's step-by-step guidance assures your grief will become not only bearable but can also become a catalyst for inspired living with time, support, and intentionality.

But, like me, you may feel resistance to healing. I hold my grief close, as a measure of my love. I want grief to have a home in my heart. I want to make my husband's life matter more than his death, and I hold on tightly to him even now. Yet I still feel comfort, rather than resistance, as I read the pages of this book. I am accepted for who I am as a griever without judgment, with both acknowledgement and understanding. I am surrounded with solace and hope as I move forward with my husband's love ever present.

When people we love die, we don't know how to live without them. We don't know who we are anymore. We wonder if we are doing something wrong. *The Sudden Loss Survival Guide* not only tackles the tough questions (How will I get through grief? How long will grief last? Am I going crazy?) but also gives you answers to normalize your grief experience.

To describe this beautiful book in a few words is impossible. Yet, it's about love. Not only love for those that have died but also love for yourself. The book teaches you how to pay tribute to your beloved person's life by honoring yourself. My husband loved life, and I want to live double now—for him and for me. I want him to be proud of the life I am living for us.

I am a living example that ordinary people can do extraordinary things if they are given the tools and guidance they need. *The Sudden Loss Survival Guide* offers you just that. My broken bits have made an exquisite mosaic over the years. Bits still fall off from time to time, and some pieces remain forever lost. I am not the same person I was before. I am shaped by both my husband's love and his death. Ten years after his death, I have rebuilt a magical life full of productive and happy moments, while allowing a place for my sorrow.

Chelsea writes, "I am healed, and you can be too," and this book serves as your guide.

—Jan Warner, author of *Grief Day by Day*

Introduction

Start Healing After Sudden Loss

I see you. I hear you. I know you.

You can't imagine your life without your loved one. You feel so deeply saddened by this sudden loss and perhaps angry at the same time. Your world does not make sense.

Your heart is hurting.

How could this happen? And why?

Like you, people I loved died.

I lost both my dad and my mom suddenly. And when I was young.

My heart, my spirit, my life was broken.

It's taken me years to work out the answers.

And I don't want you to struggle like I have.

You may:

- Miss the person who died so much that you wonder how you will go on
- Feel alone, empty, hopeless, or overwhelmed
- Wonder if your deep pain, sadness, or tears will ever stop
- Feel like you are going crazy or falling apart
- Wonder why no one understands, gets it, or feels the same
- Suffer from exhaustion, sleepless nights, and physical pains
- Experience regret, guilt, or anger
- Grapple with the unsettling questions of "Why?" "If I had?" and "Now what?"
- Feel frightened about the future and unsure about what to do next

There is hope.

You don't have to go it alone.

Help is here.

On your own terms. In your own way.

You hold in your hands a book of comfort and healing with a message of transformation embedded within it. It's ultimately the guide I wish I had had when my parents died— without warning.

I learned—all too often and all too soon—the reality of death when I was only four years old. Just before I started kindergarten, my father died unexpectedly. My mother was left alone to raise me, run my father's business, and cope with sorrow from his unanticipated death. Years later, unexpected loss struck again, bringing me to my knees when my mother died suddenly at what was supposed to be the happiest time of year—Christmas. I was only twenty-eight.

This felt like an assault on my soul and crushed my expectations about life.

As the world moved forward, I was frozen in time, brokenhearted, and shattered.

I was wounded, weak, and afraid.

It was not supposed to be this way.

I didn't want to go on.

I knew my parents would wish more for me, so I held on.

But I learned to...

- Hide my emotions
- Stuff my feelings
- Numb myself
- Pretend everything is okay

I learned how not to grieve.

I fell prey to the unrealistic expectations that mourning should be done quietly, efficiently, and quickly. I was encouraged by well-meaning people, who knew nothing about healing to "move on" and "be strong." I followed the cultural "rules" about how grief is "supposed" to be handled, and it wasn't working.

My grief and love were being minimized by these societal messages. I was being shamed to stay in quiet pain.

I was not okay. And I wanted that to be okay.

There had to be a different approach to heal my grieving heart.

I was on a quest to heal. I wanted to live my life fully in honor of those I love who had died.

I began to replace unhelpful societal information on how to grieve with natural, authentic guidance from my heart and soul.

I studied the most effective holistic healing methods of reconciling and transcending grief with skillful mentors to come to a new appreciation of life and living in "the now."

I taught myself to face my grief directly. I opened my heart to the healing powers of eternal love. I allowed myself to be supported by those who understood and acknowledged my pain. I chose my response to loss.

I grieved fully—to heal fully—to live fully.

The death of those I love changed me forever. With this real pain came real transformation. I became more open, loving, and braver than before. I discovered the depths of love. I found my true self in the pieces of my shattered heart.

My brokenness was a catalyst for transformation into wholeness—to my authentic self.

I said yes to living again.

And you can do the same.

Healing is possible.

This Is a Book of Healing

The Sudden Loss Survival Guide gives you the needed answers to many of the significant, unfamiliar challenges of living with the sudden death of the person you love.

This healing book will help you to not only work through profound sadness and deep pain, but also claim a life of meaning and happiness in honor of your beloved.

You'll receive immediate, effective, and inspiring solutions to heal sorrow while keeping the memory and spirit of your beloved person close. You'll learn the must-know practices to start to heal from sudden loss now and in the days ahead. You'll begin to live with more love, joy, and purpose, despite the tremendous challenges of sudden loss.

In the pages of this book, you'll discover how to:

- Survive, heal, and even grow from the unexpected death of someone you love

- Experience less emotional pain and regain a sense of well-being
- Develop new skills, find different perspectives, and cultivate life-affirming beliefs to cope with loss
- Recover your true, authentic self and recreate a life worth living

This Is a Book of Transformation

The death of someone you care about is a powerful catalyst for change. Your life was cracked open, inviting you to become who you were meant to be. You will be uncovering the truth of who you really are and what you truly want.

This book offers you the Seven Grief Healing Practices, which is a process to transform, heal, and transcend grief over time. The Seven Grief Healing Practices empower you with a guidance system of seven important practices to move from deep sorrow to insightful healing.

Through education, understanding, and acknowledgement of the grief process, along with your desire for healing, you will rebuild a life worth living.

As you read this book, you'll enter the powerful flow of healing to begin living again. This book gives you a path from loss and emptiness into wholeness, teaching you not only how to survive grief, but also adapt and evolve.

With this healing book as your companion, you'll have the necessary knowledge, guidance, and daily practices to reimagine life and live a meaningful, enjoyable life in honor of those you miss and love.

This Is a Book of Comfort

You will find reassuring comfort in the pages of this book as you grieve. You'll read my story and the lessons of others to see healing amidst the pain. As I wrote this book, I was thinking about you and your heartache and wanted to give you a calming balm to soothe your soul. In the pages of this comforting companion:

- You'll find hope when you lack faith.
- You'll find courage when you are afraid.
- You'll find acknowledgement when you need understanding.
- You'll find encouragement when you are downhearted.
- You'll find love when you need support.
- You'll find friendship when you desire companionship.
- You'll find meaning when you need clarity.
- You'll find navigation when you lack direction.
- You'll find truth when you want guidance.

I'm here to light a path in the darkness of your sorrow. I'm here to serve as your caring companion as you travel through the new, uncharted territory of living with the death of someone you love. I'm here for you.

When you need solace and support in the days ahead, lean on the wisdom in these pages. Consider it a gift of love, support, and compassion from my heart to yours.

How to Use This Book

The Sudden Loss Survival Guide is a book of healing, transformation, and comfort.

Keep the book close to you for easy access. You may want to establish a time each day to read an excerpt when you're waking up, going to bed, or taking a break during the day. You may want to read a little as your energy allows or dive in depending on how you're feeling. You may want to refer to the book again and again on certain days.

The book can be read from cover to cover for an overview of the grief healing process. Alternately, you can skim the book for immediate, usable tools for your current challenge or browse the book for inspiration.

If you are unsure where to start, randomly open the book and stop on a passage. You'll have likely chosen the right message to provide hope, faith, or comfort for the current moment. Embrace the words that resonate with you. Let them gently sink into your thoughts, and mark them to revisit.

The Seven Grief Healing Practices

The book's in-depth, seven-part process, the Seven Grief Healing Practices, gives the essential information and needed action to survive the devastating impact of unexpected loss.

Each of the practices takes you through the inner work of grieving and the outer work of mourning to cope with and heal from sudden loss.

Each chapter is easy to understand and builds upon the previous ones, guiding you from readjusting from sudden loss to reinvesting in life. Every chapter is organized by healing concepts, action exercises, and reflection questions.

Each of the seven chapters in this book corresponds to one of the Seven Grief Healing Practices, which are:

- Grief Healing Practice One: Readjust— Understand Sorrow
- Grief Healing Practice Two: Release—Allow and Let Go of Grief
- Grief Healing Practice Three: Renew—Foster a Support System
- Grief Healing Practice Four: Reconnect—Develop Ongoing Spiritual Connection
- Grief Healing Practice Five: Reassess—Discover Meaning and Purpose from Loss
- Grief Healing Practice Six: Reassure—Provide Peace to Those You Love
- Grief Healing Practice Seven: Remember—Honor Your Beloved and Memories Creatively

In Chapter One, Readjust—Understanding Sorrow, you'll discover how to adapt to your new circumstances and set the foundation for healing with essential information and answers to tough questions. This chapter presents the grief basics— how to adjust, what to expect, and how to make life easier—to empower you with knowledge to begin healing.

In Chapter Two, Release—Allow and Let Go of Grief, you'll learn how to become aware of and relinquish painful emotions with healthy grieving. The chapter explains how to guide healing with intention, commitment, and proactive mourning. You'll be encouraged to follow your authentic, natural progression toward healing by focusing on what helps instead of what hurts.

In Chapter Three, Renew—Foster a Support System, you'll discover renewal by using self-care and developing an effective support system. You'll learn to act as an advocate for your unique needs and become aware of the many misconceptions that do not assist healing so that you can replace them with affirming beliefs.

In Chapter Four, Reconnect—Develop Ongoing Spiritual Connection, you'll explore how to nurture the connection with the deceased by cultivating a continuing spiritual relationship. Solace and comfort are received from the redefined, evolving relationship with your loved one in order to cope with daily life and ease the transition into the future. You'll use the unbreakable spiritual bond of love to heal.

In Chapter Five, Reassess—Discover Meaning and Purpose from Loss, you'll explore the loss of a beloved person as a catalyst for life change and evaluation. You'll discover how to rebuild and reengage in life to find renewed significance and fulfillment despite the devastation of loss.

In Chapter Six, Reassure—Provide Peace to Those You Love, you'll be shown how to reveal your heart to make your love, wishes, and legacy known to your family. You'll learn to preserve your wisdom, beliefs, and values for your family and future generations. Though embracing loss, you are encouraged to embrace life.

In Chapter Seven, Remember—Cherish and Honor Memories Creatively, you'll discover how to reflect upon the past and simultaneously find comfort in the present while keeping your beloved person close in daily life. This chapter introduces creative ways and personal approaches to cherish a loved one's life and treasure memories. You'll begin to use remembering activities to heal.

Practicing What You Learn

Throughout the book, you will be given guided practices to do the work of actively releasing your grief. The exercises are tangible, concrete actions to do in order to move toward healing.

Consider putting into action what you learn as you read through the book. Incorporate the suggested healing practices and skills into your life. As you continue to use the practices, you will experience moments of joy that will continue to grow longer and more frequent. Although the outside world will not change, you will. Miraculous shifts in your perception will occur.

Read this book with an open mind toward healing. Since you are reading this book, a part of you already believes that healing after sudden loss is possible. Your desire for healing has power. Let that part of you grow and expand. Your intention to heal creates that reality. What you put into the healing process is what you'll receive in return.

You are the creator of your experience as an active, not passive, participant in your grief healing. Working through sorrow takes work and is likely the hardest task you'll ever do, but the outcome will be worth the effort—a life where you thrive and not just survive.

The skills and practices presented in *The Sudden Loss Survival Guide* are learnable. And once you have them, they will serve you for the rest of your life for any loss. When you integrate what you learn into daily life, you'll do transformative work of healing.

Noticing Resistance to Healing

At times, especially if you are new to loss, you may resist certain practices or suggestions in this book. When you are stronger or further along in grief, consider revisiting the exercises and examining if there's now a possibility for healing or a change in perspective.

You may want to turn away from your grief and ignore it. Unfortunately, time alone does not heal grief. It's what you do with your time that provides healing. It's the work you do between the minutes that allows healing. Without taking regular, manageable action to mourn and resolve grief, you can become consumed by sorrow rather than heal.

Remember that learning how to heal from grief does not mean forgetting or letting go of your beloved and his or her love. Your love grows stronger, deeper, and closer as you heal. Memories and love remain as sorrow subsides.

If you chose not to address your grief, you could:

- Lose years of your precious life stuck and overwhelmed in sorrow
- Experience continued emptiness, sadness, and pain that could've been prevented
- Settle for a life that doesn't honor your true potential
- Go from looking forward in life to just not caring anymore
- Believe your life no longer has meaning or purpose, and you can't see any way out of your situation

I don't want this for you. The people who care about you don't want this for you. The person you love who died doesn't want this for you.

Don't quit on yourself.

Don't let grief define you.

Don't give up on healing.

Yes, it will take courage, fortitude, and action. You are worth it. Your life is worth it. Your future joy is worth it. Stick with me and use this book as your trusted companion when you want to give up. Together, we'll heal grief moment by moment, page by page, and tear by tear.

It's my honor to be with you on this healing journey. If at any point, you feel you need personalized grief support, reach out to me at www.chelseahanson.com.

Now, let's activate the sacred part of you that believes healing can occur. It's time to begin the work of healing.

Starting a Dedicated Healing Journal

First, find and dedicate a journal to record your thoughts and reflections as you read this book. A notebook, pad of paper, or standard journal will do. The important part is to get started. Keep your grief healing journal in a safe, private place that is easily accessible in order to write without hesitation.

Use your journal to complete the healing practices and reflective questions in this book, and note any especially helpful information. Be honest, vulnerable, and authentic in your responses. Don't censor, judge, or stop your flow of thoughts.

If you are unsure how to begin the first entry in your healing journal, start with "I never thought I'd be writing in a grief journal. But here I am. You have died and I am grieving. As I write my thoughts and feelings, I am remembering you."

Consider keeping your book and journal in the same place in your home so it doesn't get misplaced. If at times you don't have your journal, give yourself freedom to write in this book, take notes, and highlight passages that resonate with you. This will make it easier to find the information you'd like to apply or review.

Creating a Safe Place to Grieve

Next, let's create a safe, sacred space for you to grieve and heal. As you read this book, each day you'll be learning more about healing grief, coping strategies, and the many ways you're in control of your thoughts, actions, and future. To get beyond grief, you must go through it, not around it.

That means you'll need a healing sanctuary, a place of quiet, calm solitude, to honor grief and allow your feelings. Everyone does. It's important to have a "safe place" to cry, reflect, relax, and just "be" in order to experience and express emotions. Find yours. It might be the couch in your den, a soft chair by a sunny window, or a cheery patio or nook in your garden. Your bed might be the safest place for you, propped up on pillows, surrounded by what you need to heal. Others find comfort in a man cave, a workshop, or a craft or sewing room.

You may prefer getting outside, being in nature, sitting in your garden, or going for a short walk, bike ride, or canoe outing as a way to get your body and emotions moving. A safe place for you might even be inside your car, parked next to a nurturing place, within a stand of trees, or alongside an open meadow, lake, or pond. Choose whatever space feels comfortable and inviting. Ideally, it should be a place with no phones, interruptions, televisions, nor family members—a place and time set apart only for you. View this as your "healing sanctuary" or "sacred space" to be alone with yourself and your sorrow to seek peace and renewal.

Give this designated space a meaningful or enjoyable name. You can even name it after your loved one, such as Collin's Cubby, Sarah's Loft, or Noel's Nook. Be creative, and choose a name that sparks joy in your spirit. Avoid names that may bring more dread or sadness. If you can't think of a title, rest assured, you'll come up with one soon. If not, it's perfectly fine to forgo naming your sacred space.

Making Your Healing Sanctuary Meaningful

To make your healing sanctuary an inviting place for your mind, body, and soul, add soothing items to increase serenity and peacefulness for all five senses. Consider flowers, soft music, or light fragrance. Add a fountain, plants, crystals, or inspiring wall décor. The sounds, smells, and textures can soothe your aching heart and body.

To make your sacred space more expressive, surround yourself with family pictures, meaningful mementos, and items symbolic of your relationship with your beloved person. Encircle yourself with things that calm your heart and lift your spirit. To add inspiration, display uplifting quotes, add a favorite mantra of the person you miss, or showcase a sentimental object that reminds you of the deceased's values, characteristics, or legacy.

Choose items to bring joy rather than sadness. If items from your loved one do not bring comfort, do not include them in your sanctuary. As your healing progresses, physical reminders of the person you miss may bring solace and can be added at that time.

My current healing space is in my office, behind closed doors. I am surrounded by lovely framed pictures of deceased loved ones, dear friends, and pets. The ashes of my husband's brother rest on a special shelf. I see meaningful mementos, including a framed drawing my mother made when she was only fifteen, dried flowers from a special family event, and photos of childhood memories with my parents. I burn fragrant candles and use a diffuser for essential oils.

Using Your Healing Sanctuary

Use this quiet place to retreat to each day for about ten to fifteen minutes. This healing space will be your safe haven, a place away from the world. You can rest here after a long workday, a sleepless night, a burst of tears, or a rough trip out into the world.

Here you can continue to release sorrow and be alone with your thoughts. You do not need to edit or judge your feelings— just be wherever you are. When you let your guard down and allow emotions to surface, you invite grief to flow through you, including the most painful aspects you normally want to avoid.

Enter your healing sanctuary for only a short time daily because it can be more bearable to feel your sorrow in small doses. Here you can safely think about the person you love, what he or she means to you, and how you feel about his or her physical absence. Entering your sanctuary can also provide time to address other areas of your life that need attention, such as changes in income, living arrangements, or family interactions.

During your time in your safe haven, you can open your heart to what you're experiencing and safely give yourself permission to grieve. You might:

- Light a candle
- Pray
- Meditate

- Cry
- Read
- Listen to music (your favorites or your loved one's favorites)
- Use movement through dance or song
- Imagine your loved one
- Speak your truth
- Express your love
- Share unsaid messages
- Write in your dedicated grief healing journal

Visit your healing sanctuary daily, if possible, especially early in your grief, because it gives you a cue that this is the time to honor and express feelings freely. You'll regularly allow emotions to move through your body and release them privately while in your safe haven.

Make it a ritual to visit your sanctuary, which is your special refuge from the world—a place where you give yourself love, freedom, and rest. Here you can find comfort and solace in your bereavement.

Practice One

Readjust: Understand Sorrow

Journey through Grief

"We live in a world that doesn't like pain. We, too, might be
tempted to turn from it, to keep a stiff upper lip. But grief asks
us to touch pain, to sit with pain, to ask it to tea. Being with
your sorrow is brave. It is counter-culture courage."

—Ashley Davis Bush

A sudden destruction of your world has occurred. Someone
you love was taken without warning. Your life changed in an
instant. Your world shattered into a million little pieces. You
are unprepared and can't believe what is happening. Sudden
loss brings you to your knees. You need support, compassion,
and love as you adjust.

You are not alone. This book will serve as a caring friend,
trusted companion, and wisdom-filled guide to help you
through your grief. The answers *you* seek are here. You'll
receive inspiration, understanding, encouragement, and
empowering practices to survive heartbreak, and transform
it into a life-affirming commitment to greater love, joy,
and authenticity.

Your journey through grief is like no other. Your loss is
uniquely yours because it's about the distinct relationship
you have with the person who died. Yet, because you're
experiencing loss, you'll find comfort here in knowing how
other survivors have adjusted and navigated this journey.

At first, you have these overwhelming feelings of loss and
grief. The sadness is heavy and unbearable. You are riding
on a debilitating roller coaster of despair, rage, disbelief,
and sleepless nights. You wonder if your pain will ever end.

You question why no one understands and what to do next. Focusing on anything—anything at all, let alone meaningful—seems impossible.

This is normal.

You're grieving and you're allowed to...no, encouraged to grieve. Give yourself permission to mourn in your own way.

You're filled with questions.

How can I go on?

How will I adjust?

What will my life be like going forward?

So much clouds your mind, making it difficult to concentrate. So many frightening questions with no real answers, until now. Questions you never imagined you'd have to ask. Losing someone you love will alter your life forever.

The first essential practice to begin to heal grief is to readjust by understanding sorrow. Here's what you need to know:

Healing is possible. Grief is a process—a journey that continues. It's not something you'll get over and then be "back to normal" in no time. When someone you care about dies, you may feel an unending sense of loss. But *you* get to decide what the grieving experience looks and feels like and—believe it or not—healing can be transformative as you identify new priorities and meaning in your life.

You cannot control losing those you love, but you can consciously guide how you respond to your loss and how you deal with sorrow. I did not learn this lesson until many years after my mother died suddenly when I was only twenty-eight years old. I had mistakenly believed grief was something that passively descended upon me, not knowing I could take steps to heal from loss.

I stayed stuck, and I carried old, unhealed losses and emotions for years. My father had died unexpectedly, at age forty-one, due to complications from heart surgery when I was only four. As a young adult, I didn't consider the possibility that I could lose Mom, too. I had a warped sense of security. *What would be the possibility that I would lose a second parent? The odds are in my favor, right?*

Wrong. Death is real. Another parent died. It shook me to my core. It seemed like I was in a slow-motion film that kept running, and I couldn't escape the nightmare. Suddenly, nothing else mattered. Loss made me realize how fragile and precious life is—how everything can change in a moment and never be the same.

When death struck, I lost a part of myself, a piece of my past, and a vision for my future. I wasn't going to be the person I was before loss. Instead, I would be different with a new normal. Others wanted me to return to the old me, but this wasn't possible.

Someone I loved died, and I was cracked wide open. My heart, my spirit, and my life were shattered. My brokenness was a catalyst for personal transformation—once I gained the tools and resources to work with it.

When the raw pain is so unbearable and unbelievable, you may wonder if you can go on. But you can, and you will. And life can be good again—*when* you work at it. It's a conscious choice to decide to move through grief, mourn the loss of the person you love, and heal.

Be patient with yourself as you find your way through unfamiliar emotions. Pace yourself. Give yourself all the time and freedom you need to walk with grief, rather than run away. Your job right now is to take good care of yourself, be gentle with yourself, and take it slow.

Allow yourself to grieve in your own way, not how others would like you to. Deep down inside, you already know how to mourn if you let yourself. Offer yourself what you need moment by moment to move toward living again. Allow yourself to readjust emotionally, spiritually, and physically. Follow your natural, organic inclinations toward healing rather than trying to obey unrealistic expectations from yourself or others.

Can you open your heart to the natural human process of grieving?

How Will I Get through Loss?

"Most people do not know how brave they really are."

—R.E. Chambers

Sorrow has turned your world upside down. Nothing feels right. Nothing feels good. Nothing is the same. The loss is ever-present and feels so achingly unbearable. You feel empty, alone, and lost.

You do not need to do anything initially. Take it minute by minute, hour by hour, and day by day. As the hours add up to a day, you'll have accomplished what may have seemed impossible. When you make it through one day, you can get through another. You do not need to look ahead. Focus on the present and continue to breathe.

I remember being surprised that I could still breathe despite missing Mom so much. I thought my heart would surely stop beating, but I surprisingly continued to wake up each morning. When thinking back to losing Dad, I was equally astonished that Mom could go on after his death. I can only imagine how helpless, exhausted, and vulnerable she must have felt.

About three weeks after Mom died, the shock and numbness began to wear off. The stark reality of the situation settled in. I did not want to go on. I yearned for her so much that I simply wanted to leave the physical world to be with her. My mother was my person. She had gone home, and I wanted to return home also. I could not fathom any other answer to my unbearable pain.

Somehow, I continued to breathe. The intensity of the feelings moved through me again and again, day after day, and week after week. My heart kept beating. My body kept aching. My mind kept trying to find a way out of the pain.

Although it may not seem fathomable right now, you will heal and find the resilience you need to move through this life-changing time. Others have done it, and you can, too. I'll guide you through the essential healing practices as you continue to read chapters two through seven.

How can you find solace in the present moment?

What Grief Is

"The agony is great… And yet I will stand it. Had I not loved
so very much I would not hurt so much. But goodness knows I
would not want to diminish that precious love by one fraction
of an ounce. I will hurt, and I will be grateful to the hurt for it
bears witness to the depth of our meanings, and for that I will
be eternally grateful."

–Dr. Elisabeth Kübler-Ross

Grief is an authentic reaction to loving. If you had not loved
so deeply, you would not grieve so deeply. Only a person who
is incapable of love is entirely free of the possibility of sorrow.
Grief and love are inextricably intertwined.

Sorrow highlights your deep capacity to love and be loved. Grief
is loss in love—continuing to love the person who died, but
understanding his or her human presence is gone. We may not
understand the depth and magnitude of love until physical loss
occurs. You will love in separation.

Like you, I grieve for the people I miss due to the strong love I
have for them today, tomorrow, and always. I would never give
up the experience of loving them to avoid the pain of losing
them. My deceased loved ones are mine forever—in heart,
spirit, and mind—and our love grows stronger, deeper, and
more profound. Sorrow only exists where love first lived.

How is your sorrow like love?

What Grief Is Not

Grief is not a disease, a mental or emotional disorder, a bad attitude or perspective, or a misbehavior or sin. Grief does not need to be cured, diagnosed and medicated out of existence, fixed, recovered from, or avoided. Grieving people are not sick, broken, or crazy. Mourners are simply experiencing a natural, human response to the loss of a person due to death.

—Larry Barber, The Grief Minister

Grief is *not* a disease that can be "cured" or an illness to "get over." Grief is composed of the internal thoughts and feelings you experience in response to loss. Processing your grief is necessary, and it is often referred to as "grief work." As you mourn, which means to outwardly express and release your grief, you'll learn to adapt to and incorporate the loss of a beloved person into your life.

Time alone will not heal grief. Perhaps, it may soften or even dull your pain; however, it is what you *do* with time that is important. Time along with effort, the intention to heal, and the conscious action to mourn will gradually bring peace instead of pain.

An active, not passive, approach to your healing is essential. You do not heal grief by only waiting for something to happen. You must honor, process, and integrate your feelings and emotions if you desire healing.

Like any other deep wound, mending cannot be rushed, and you must lovingly tend to your profound sorrow. When you postpone or ignore grief, you block your future capacity for aliveness. You could be consumed by sorrow, rather than heal as you are meant to. Instead, allow the natural flow of healing little by little—experience the emotional ups and downs, the ebbs and flows, and the intensity and calm.

It's likely you've heard about the five stages of grief described by Dr. Elisabeth Kübler-Ross in her 1969 book, *On Death & Dying*.[i] During her observation of terminally ill patients, she identified a series of emotions they experienced as they faced their own impending death. Unfortunately, these stages have been incorrectly applied to mourners, when this was not Dr. Kübler-Ross's intent. Many people have misconstrued her model to suggest grief can be cured by progressing through these sequential, universally identifiable stages: denial, anger, bargaining, depression, and acceptance.

Do not try to fit your mourning experience into neat, logical stages. Healing from grief is not a rigid framework to be followed. Instead, grief can be, and often is, one of the least predictable and rational experiences you will ever go through. Working through grief is not the smooth, straight progression that most people initially assume.

Don't burden yourself with thoughts of grieving "the right way." There is no correct or incorrect way. There are many theories about grief, and some may accurately describe your experience, and some may not. Either way, it does not mean there is something wrong with you.

The next chapter shows you how to actively grieve in ways that align with your feelings and natural inclinations. You'll discover how to apply what is correct for your personal circumstances to experience less emotional pain and regain well-being.

Can you allow your natural healing progression to begin?

How Long Will Grief Last?

"You will heal, and you will rebuild yourself around the loss
you have suffered. You will be whole again, but you will
never be the same. Nor should you be the same, nor would
you want to."

—Elisabeth Kübler-Ross

"Isn't it time you let go?"

"Shouldn't you be over it by now?"

You may hear these questions from others and know they
reflect the misconception that there is an acceptable amount
of time to grieve. However, your sorrow is unique to you, your
relationship with your loved one, and the circumstances of
death. The intensity and duration of grief varies. Do not let
others persuade you to think differently.

Sorrow doesn't follow any timeline. There are no shortcuts or
quick fixes. You cannot predict how you may feel in the future
or follow set timetables. Just because an established amount of
time has passed does not mean you will feel a certain way. Grief
is not bound by time.

Most people expect grief to be over within a year, at the most. I
also believed this myth. It took more than three years until my
mother's death didn't dominate my waking thoughts. Morning
after morning and month after month, I woke up feeling fine
for a few seconds until I remembered my current reality. I
wanted to go back into my dream state, so I could forget that
someone I love had died and would not be coming back.

The only people who think there is a timeline to grief healing have not experienced unexpected loss. Unfortunately for mourners, those who have not lost a piece of their heart expect sudden loss survivors to be back to "normal" within a few weeks or months. This is not realistic.

Others may encourage you to suppress your sorrow due to their own discomfort and helplessness surrounding grief. They don't want you to be in pain, but don't know how to help. They may not want to feel their own uncomfortable feelings. Thus, others may pressure you to "move on" and "get back to normal." You may be encouraged to "get over" your grief and "speed up" your recovery, but your healing will not have a timeline.

Friends may urge you to keep busy. Not knowing what else to do, you may heed this advice. But, by moving away from your pain, you are prolonging suffering and risk carrying unresolved grief forward into the years ahead. Long-term relief is not found when underlying feelings are not addressed.

Others should not expect you to be the same as you were before. Life changes you, whatever the experience. For example, you are not an identical person after getting married, having children, getting divorced, or switching careers. Similarly, you are irrevocably changed and transformed by sudden loss and will form a new understanding of life, meaning, and purpose.[ii]

You will heal in your own time and readjust to life gradually as a changed person. You will not be the person you were before. How could you be? You will have expanded your capacity to grow, love, and thrive in the face of previously unimaginable pain.

You will live beside sorrow as you merge sudden loss into your life. Speaking from my own experience and that of many others, you will learn to live with the physical loss of the person you love. This doesn't imply you'll never be joyful again, nor able to step forward. It simply means that your loved one will continue to be important in a different way.

Just as you were changed by being loved by this special person in your life, you will be impacted by the loss. You will miss your beloved every day of your life but will learn to live on fully in honor of his or her memory. "At some point your grief will end, but this doesn't mean that there will ever be an end to the sense of loss," Helen Fitzgerald wrote so eloquently.[iii]

Can you respect the unique length of your healing?

What Should I Expect?

"It's a passage, not a place to stay."

–Lois Wyse

Grief is the hardest work you'll ever do. You are irreversibly changed and transformed by sudden loss, but you can move beyond sorrow to form a new understanding of life, love, and fulfillment. You will not return to where you started.

You've moved into a different world with unpredictability and chaos. Unexpected loss bewilders, upsets, and frightens anyone living with it. It's unquestionably one of the most difficult journeys you will ever face. Bereavement involves tears, unfathomable pain, and overwhelming sorrow. You may experience shock, numbness, disbelief, disorganization, confusion, anxiety, panic, fear, explosive emotions, guilt, regret, emptiness, and sadness.

In addition to the debilitating emotions and unfamiliar feelings, you can suffer physical ailments. I experienced migraine headaches, weight loss, and sleep disturbances for many months after Mom died. The physical effects of grief surprised me, especially since I had not previously suffered any prolonged physical illness. One of my clients was equally surprised when I explained her stomach pains and nausea could be grief manifesting in her body while her husband went through chemotherapy. Her physical reactions were sympathetic symptoms to what her husband experienced.

Everyone grieves and reacts differently. According to J. William Worden's *Tasks of Mourning*,[iv] there are four major components of grief work:

- to accept the reality of loss
- to process the pain of grief
- to adjust to a world without the deceased
- to find an enduring connection with the deceased while embarking on a new life

The tasks aren't sequential, and you may oscillate among the four. You're adjusting to a forever-altered life, and you are already doing the work of grieving. As you continue to actively mourn your sudden loss, you will begin to heal in your own way. If you do not complete the tasks of mourning, healing will take longer and effectively integrating loss into your life may not occur.

What tasks of mourning are you experiencing?

Am I Going Crazy?

"At other times it feels like being mildly drunk, or concussed.
There is a sort of invisible blanket between the world and me.
I find it hard to take in what anyone says. Or perhaps, hard to
want to take it in. It is so uninteresting. Yet I want the others to
be about me. I dread the moments when the house is empty.
If only they would talk to one another and not to me."

—C. S. Lewis

Feeling like you're going crazy or that you're losing it is a very
common emotion after a sudden loss, but it doesn't mean that
it's true. You're experiencing unfamiliar feelings and emotions
and may question their validity and soundness because you've
never experienced anything like unexpected death before.

Sudden loss of a loved one is traumatic. It can leave you
feeling lost or not knowing what to do. You may feel confused
and unable to make decisions. Some people describe feeling
like they are in a daze. Some are unable to cry, while others
sob. Forgetfulness, brain fog, and clumsiness are commonly
experienced after an unexpected death.

When I returned to work two weeks after Mom died, I was
unable to concentrate on a difficult and large project that was
assigned to me. I tried and tried to study the new material.
But I just couldn't concentrate. *What is the matter with me?
Why can't I just do what I was supposed to?* My supervisor
had assumed I would be back to normal and could handle this
unusual task. But that wasn't the case. After being back at my
job for a few days, I had to take two months off to tend to my
powerful, all-consuming sorrow. I had no choice but to turn

inward, honor my deep sorrow, and find a new home for my unexpected emotions.

Feeling out of sorts is one of the many ways you might grieve, and it is perfectly acceptable. These feelings are normal and are not permanent.

Simply said, you're not going crazy; you're grieving.

Don't apologize for your feelings or tears. They are a natural part of the process, and you have the right to experience them in public or private.

Releasing emotions through tears allows you to feel better. Moving toward pain instead of away from it allows healing. Tension and anxiety flow out of your body. Society may view tears as a sign of weakness and inadequacy; however, the courageous heart shows emotion and expresses the need to be comforted by others. Crying is how your heart speaks. The person who died is worthy of as many tears as you can cry.

Know that these seemingly crazy and unusual feelings will not last forever. As the pain softens, you'll discover hope. When you give yourself permission to feel your sorrow, healing begins and love wins.

How might you focus on yourself right now?

Why Don't Others Talk about Death?

"When a person is born, we rejoice, and when they're married, we jubilate, but when they die, we pretend nothing happened."

–Margaret Mead

Most people don't like to talk or think about loss because they fear it. They don't want to admit unexpected death will happen or that it's real. Western society likes to keep the thought of dying at a distance because most people don't want to be reminded of their mortality.

It wasn't always this way, but twenty-first-century culture perpetuates denial and avoidance of grief. By contrast, our ancestors were more enlightened. They honored their loved ones in death, privately and publicly, through rituals. Past generations wore symbols of bereavement, used designated time periods for mourning, and relied on nearby family and close-knit communities for support. Because of lower life expectancies than we have today, they often experienced personal losses at a young age. Death was part of everyday life, and families were familiar with societal rituals and practices to care for the bereaved.

But today, people haven't learned how to talk about dying or how to support the bereaved. Due to this lack of education and fear, you may be hesitant to talk about your loss and how much it changes your life.

Allow all your responses and feelings, not just those you view as acceptable. Friends and family may unknowingly share grief misconceptions, give misguided advice, and encourage you to shorten your mourning experience. Like me, you may have unknowingly internalized the message that grieving should be done quietly, quickly, and efficiently. I pretended to be okay to fit the expectations of others, but when I was alone, I knew differently. I learned that imposing unrealistic expectations on myself about how to mourn deters healing.

Let others know it's okay to discuss sudden loss, dying, and the life and death of your loved one. By being aware of society's lack of grief education and discomfort with death, you can guide conversations away from unhelpful information toward asking for the support you need. If you don't share what you need and expect from others, this can impede your healing.

Take the initiative to start a conversation about what you want to support your healing. Chapter Three provides helpful guidance on how to develop a support system that works for you. You'll discover how to serve as an advocate for your unique needs and wants.

How can you guide others to support you?

Should I Talk about Her/Him?

"The mention of my child's name may bring tears to my eyes, but it never fails to bring music to my ears."

—Anonymous

Talk about your loved one. One of the topics that comes up most often during my healing grief workshops or during my coaching work with clients is the question: how do I share memories of my loved one?

If you are wondering the same thing, then openly share memories, feelings, and sorrow. Don't be afraid to mention your beloved's name or worry about how others will react. Say his or her name in everyday conversations. View it as a privilege and responsibility to keep your loved one's memory alive in daily life.

Some people fear talking about the deceased will upset others, so they remain quiet. However, others may want to talk, but don't know what to say to start the conversation. If that is the case, let those around you know that it's okay to discuss your loved one and that you welcome it.

I love when my stepfather mentions my mother's name, Donna, as he is one of the few people who says her name. Others refer to my mother as "your mom" or don't mention her at all, so it is a wonderful feeling to hear Mom's first name spoken many years after her death.

How can you include your beloved in everyday conversations?

Where Is My Loved One?

"Do not stand at my grave and weep,
I am not there; I do not sleep.
I am a thousand winds that blow,
I am the diamond glints on snow,
I am the sun on ripened grain,
I am the gentle autumn rain.
When you awaken in the morning's hush,
I am the swift uplifting rush
Of quiet birds in circled flight.
I am the soft star-shine at night.
Do not stand at my grave and cry,
I am not there; I did not die."

—Mary Elizabeth Frye

You may be wondering:

Where is my loved one?

Is he or she alright?

Is my beloved in heaven?

It's normal to ponder where your dear one is now. It doesn't matter if you are religious or spiritual; most mourners believe people who die still exist in some form. Experts agree that after a person dies, we continue in another form of energy, and it is through this energy that we stay connected.

The spirit of your loved one is very much alive and with you. You may not be able to see, touch, or hold your loved one, but perhaps you believe he or she is in heaven or is a shining star. Perhaps you imagine your beloved is now surrounded by all the friends and family he or she has ever loved. Perhaps you know he or she is forever with you.

Your religious upbringing may influence what you believe. On the other hand, you don't have to be a religious person to imagine what's possible when you remain spiritually connected to your beloved.

What I know for sure:

Love never dies.

Love lives on.

Love is everlasting.

The deceased person's physical presence is no longer with you, but your relationship continues in a way based on spirit and love. "You will continue now, and forever, to redefine the relationship with your deceased loved one. Death doesn't end the relationship; it simply forges a new relationship—one not based on physical presence but on memory, spirit and love," wrote Ashley Davis Bush.[v]

Staying connected to deceased loved ones facilitates healing as well as the ability to cope with the loss and accompanying changes, according to Dennis Klass's book, *Continuing Bonds, New Understandings of Grief*.[vi] The author writes, "These 'connections' provide solace, comfort and support, and ease the transition from the past to the future."

Whatever you believe, choose thoughts and actions that bring you reassurance and comfort. There are many ways to hold onto the person who has died. You don't need to sever your relationship. Instead, you can redefine the relationship in healthy, life-affirming ways. Your love will continue for the missed person throughout your life.

Remembering your beloved can sustain you in your grief journey. Holding onto the memory of a loved one doesn't mean you are stuck. This continuing bond of love is immortal and infinite. Once you have love, you cannot lose it. It is yours always. It doesn't diminish over time, but continues to grow stronger, especially from the spiritual realm.

Love can transcend any barrier, and its purest form allows you to encompass the essence of your loved one. You may be able to see, feel, or know that this magical presence is near you.

Chapters Four and Seven provide spiritual and tangible practices to help you remember your loved one. You'll discover several creative ways to embrace memories with comfort and meaning to continue the bond of love.

How might you continue the relationship with your loved one in a new, different way?

Why Did This Happen?

"No farewell words were spoken, no time to say good-bye.
You were gone before I knew it and only God knows why.
My heart still aches in sadness and secret tears still flow,
what it meant to lose you, no one will ever know."

—Tombstone inscription

Perhaps you're asking...

Why?

Why now?

Why me?

Many tragedies defy explanation in a sometimes crazy, dark, and confusing world. Consider finding answers to questions you know can be explained. For example, if you were not with your loved one when he or she died, you may want to know the details of how and when the death occurred. Or if you were present, you may need more information to understand what happened. Collecting the missing pieces of information that are available will be integral to your healing.

Unfortunately, unanswerable questions will remain, and they are often protests in disguise.

Only you can assign meaning to an unexpected loss that has affected your soul.

You may demand answers to questions that are unanswerable. You can search and yearn for answers and still not know. Perhaps only eternity may provide true understanding. Perhaps the unexpected death is part of a higher purpose that will be uncovered in the afterlife. Perhaps your beloved will watch and care for you from another place.

There's one thing I can tell you for sure: the sudden death of the person you love is never a punishment, retribution, or retaliation for how you lived your life. Unfortunately, it is the natural course of things in the universe—a realm that will support you in your time of need.

You may have received comments from people trying to give meaning to death.

"There is a reason for everything."

"God has a plan."

"At least you got all those years with him or her."

Do not feel compelled to listen to how others respond to your grief because their answers may not be helpful. These reactions typically don't provide comfort and may anger you. Seek your own understanding and listen to your intuition.

Right now, you're facing a terrible loss. You may feel like you've lost the race of life. I promise you, in the end, you're going to be whole and win. I believe you'll be reunited with your loved one at the end of your life. You will be home, together.

If you received answers to the questions you seek, would this change how you feel?

Why Am I Questioning My Faith?

"Sorrow looks back, worry looks around, faith looks up."

—Ralph Waldo Emerson

Sudden loss, like you've experienced, changes so many things. Abruptly. So much so, you may begin to question what you thought you knew and believed. You may need to question everything and find new beliefs.

This is normal. Why?

Because you lost a piece of your heart.

You suffered an unexpected loss that will change your existence, teach you great lessons, and reveal mysteries of life.

You experienced a loss you wish wouldn't have happened and one that you couldn't control. You underwent a tragedy you would've given up everything to prevent.

Whose faith in life wouldn't be shaken by such an event?

You may not have thought about your faith as much as you do now, given your circumstance. At the same time, you've likely never felt such little faith as you do now. To believe is easy when everything is simple and stress-free, but when something bad happens, faith becomes confusing and complicated. You may need to determine if your previous beliefs still serve you now.

Some suffering is so extraordinary that even the most spiritual people wonder if their higher power cares about them or even if there is such a thing. Although I believe a universal power is near, you may sense the absence and feel alone like never before. After all, you may wonder how a higher power could allow such searing pain and terrible loss.

The presence of spirit may be closer to you now than it was ever before, but in the fog of grief, this may be difficult to feel or believe. In retrospect, I can see how the universe provided me with invisible support after my parents died, but I didn't see or recognize it at the time. How could something so terrible happen to *me*? Now, I understand. No one can escape the loss of someone they love or care about. It's a natural part of living, even though we *so* wish it weren't.

How will faith play a role in your healing?

How Do I Make Sense of This?

"We cannot understand. The best is perhaps what we understand least."

–C. S. Lewis

Your beliefs and faith are tested by death. You may be angry with your faith and doubt everything. You may grapple with changing values and priorities. When my mother was in the intensive care unit, I prayed for a miracle. And when I didn't receive it, I was angry, disappointed, and lost faith in a benevolent universe. It took me many years to come to terms with my mother's death and the seeming lack of answers to my prayers.

When you lose someone suddenly, everything changes. You now know how precious your time is while you're alive. A whole

new world of courage and possibility will open as you discover
what's important.

You'll make sense of the chaos of loss in your own way and in
your own time. It's your choice to search for and choose the
meaning *you* would like to assign to the death of your loved
one. What enduring values, beliefs, or practices have grounded
you in this tremendous turmoil? Is it your family, a spiritual
knowing, or certain surroundings? What has helped you cope?
Identify what has given you strength and continue to hold
onto that.

Chapter Five provides insight on how to find ongoing meaning
and purpose after sudden loss. You'll discover how conscious
choice and action can shape your future.

**How has your personal belief system been
challenged by loss?**

Will I Have Closure?

"You can love someone so much, but you can never love people as much as you can miss them."

—John Green

Closure is a myth in the heart of a griever. Ask any parent who has lost a child, and he or she will tell you that closure doesn't exist.

It may be healthier to think about integrating loss into your life. Although your loved one died, your relationship lives on, and you will learn how to cope in a new world. When I gave up the idea of closure, my grief softened, and a new world of possibility opened. My need to achieve closure brought me anguish, but my current desire to continue my relationships brings me relief.

Gradually, you adjust and function again. You *will* learn new ways to live with loss, communicate with your deceased loved one, and share memories. Today, I share family memories with my son, who never met my parents, so he can know and love his family even though they are not physically with him.

Rather than seeking closure, discover new ways to move forward with life and still hold your loved one forever in your heart. You will not feel sorrow forever. In fact, there will be times when you will not be consciously sad. At other times, grief and joy will exist simultaneously within you. It's okay for happiness and sorrow to sit side-by-side. You will have been shaped by all your relationships and experiences. You will have built a life on what came before.

Love and memories remain. Remember, love is forever, life after life.

How will you keep your beloved person close in daily life?

Will Happiness Ever Reappear?

"I'd like the memory of me to be a happy one.
I'd like to leave an afterglow of smiles when day is done.
I'd like to leave an echo whispering softly down the ways,
of happy times and laughing times and bright and
sunny days.
I'd like the tears of those who grieve, to dry before the sun
of happy memories I leave behind—when day is done."

–Helen Lowrie Marshall

Although it is unthinkable now, a day will come when you wake up and the death of the person you love will not be your first thought. Your profound sadness will diminish. Happiness will be yours again. You'll smile and laugh when thinking of your beloved. You'll know your loved one is still with you each new day. You'll expand your understanding about the preciousness of life and gain a new sense of joy and purpose through grief.

Twelve years ago, I told a bereaved mother, less than twenty-four hours after her one-year-old daughter's sudden death, to continue to just breathe when she didn't want to go on. Now, I delight in seeing this same woman light up with a twinkle in her eye and a smile on her face when she talks about her beautiful daughter. Thinking about this mother's face brings tears to my eyes. She did it, and you will too. Just like the countless people before you have survived, and even thrived, after the unexpected death of a beloved person.

"When you grieve fully, and when you grieve in a healthy way, the experience of loss is about more than loss. It's possible that you can come to feel that something has been added to your life, even as something has been taken away. It's possible that you'll be deepened as a person as you grieve, that your horizons in life will be widened. An expanded sense of yourself can emerge. You can become more attuned to life's meaning," explains Jim Miller.[vii]

Chapter Five provides guidance on how to rebuild and reengage in life to find renewed significance and fulfillment.

What would your deceased loved one want for your future?

Practice Two

Release: Allow and Let Go of Grief

You Can and Will Go On

"It is hard in the future, when we are temporarily just not brave enough. When this happens, concentrate on the present. Cultivate the little happiness until courage returns. Look forward to the beauty of the next moment, the next hour, the promise of a good meal, sleep, a book, a movie, the likelihood that tonight stars will shine and tomorrow the sun will shine. Sink roots into the present until the strength grows to think about tomorrow."

—Ardis Whitman

Sudden loss is unique. Nothing in life prepares you for losing someone you care about unexpectedly. The stark absence knocks the life out of you, and it's a gut-wrenching punch to the soul. Your world does not make sense. You are overwhelmed. You weren't able to anticipate or prepare for this death and the upsetting emotions.

The shock of losing someone you love without warning makes grief more difficult. Your coping capacity is diminished, and your functioning is impaired. Unlike an anticipated, expected loss, you had no time to make a gradual transition, revise your expectations, or plan for changes.

Coping with sudden loss takes resiliency, courage, and patience to heal and rebuild life. The mind wants to find a solution to make the pain go away. But you cannot think your way out of grief. You need to feel your way out of grief. Feelings need to be faced with honesty and openness to allow, express, and release them fully.

Rather than fighting your grief, allow yourself to surrender and experience your emotions completely. But how do you do that? This chapter empowers you with the information you need to know to begin to release grief by allowing and letting it go. You'll learn why you deny your emotions and how to befriend them instead.

When you are new to loss, you think it may kill you, but your body will continue to hold on. The energy that will carry you forward when you don't know if you can go on is the strength of your divine spirit, which is always with you. The universe closely holds your soul, ready to guide you back to a renewed life when you're ready and able.

When you experience the full impact of pain and finality of loss, you may feel abandoned and alone. Know that you can and will go on. You've become a member of a club that no one wants to join. If experienced grievers could give you only one piece of advice, it would be this: you'll make it through your sorrow and live again.

Try this daily grief healing practice: Comforting Your Hurting Heart. Use this opening grief healing practice to begin your time in your sanctuary, which is your peaceful, sacred space where you will go to safely grieve your hurt each day. This book's introduction shows you how to set up your healing sanctuary if you haven't already done so.

Begin your time in your sanctuary by allowing yourself to whisper these starting words, "I can and will go on," with belief. Hold this message in your mind and feel the power of this thought to truly believe it. Now, imagine your heart has a protective golden shield around it that you're opening to allow this mantra to flow through and into your heart. The deep wound in your heart allows love to flow both ways, in and out.

This is where the light enters the darkness to navigate your way home again. The very center of your heart is where healing starts and life begins again.

Feel the comforting message "I can and will go on" in your heart space. Let these loving words seep into your entire body and flow into your soul. Allow the possibility of healing to enter *all* of your being as you make the choice today to live on in honor of the person you love who died.

Is it possible to believe (even just for today) you can and will go on?

Choosing Hope

"Hope never abandons you. You abandon it."

–Ardis Whitman

You might have categorized your life into two parts—before loss and after loss.

No matter how hard things seem, continue to believe in yourself and your future. You have the ability to consciously choose and cultivate hope at any moment. Even when the challenges are unbearable, choose to hold onto hope for a reimagined future. Hope gives you the ability to rise in the morning and to know that today may be better than yesterday... and that there's possibility for an improved tomorrow.

First, believe in hope.

Second, never let it go.

Hang on when riding the rollercoaster of grief. Yell and scream all you want as you hit those curves, dips, and bumps of your sorrow, but please don't let go. Hang on...

Hang on to faith.

Hang on to love.

Hang on to memories.

Hang on to life.

You will return to living, and healing will occur. Hold on to hope that this day is coming. When you want to give up, that's the time to trust and surrender to a benevolent universe. Hope will shine light in dark moments when it's welcomed in.

I was in a grief support group a few weeks after my mother suddenly died, and a middle-aged woman who had experienced the death of her husband a year before was the special guest. The group leaders eagerly greeted her and seemed elated about her attendance. I was amazed she had reached the one-year anniversary of her spouse's death. I couldn't imagine it, but here she was, a real living person who had survived her sorrow for an unimaginable amount of time from my point of view. She provided a light and beacon of hope and didn't even know how inspirational her survival was to me and the other group members. She was healing. What was possible for her was possible for us.

Remember this simple acronym: HOPE—Hang On, Pain Ends.

Try this daily grief healing practice: Cultivating Hopeful Gratitude. Begin to foster hope today. Notice the small gifts of the day—a friend's consoling hug, the restorative power of a blue sky, the peace of a serene lake, or the laughter of a child. Notice what you take for granted that can be appreciated, such as a roof over your head, your health, or others in your life.

For tomorrow, observe one beautiful thing—perhaps a flower, a smile, or a photo. For the next day, choose what you want to see. Try to isolate an occasional wonderful moment in your daily grieving.

If you are having a hard time noticing anything to be grateful for, ask yourself, "What can I hope for now that things have changed?" Focusing on what you are thankful for brings you into the present moment, and that's where healing occurs.

Note your feelings and answers in your dedicated grief healing journal, which is your private summary of thoughts and insights for you to revisit. Setting up your grief healing journal was discussed in the book's introduction.

How can you invite hope into your life?

Committing to Healing

"The moment one definitely commits oneself, then providence moves too."

—J. W. Goethe

Commit to healing and you will.

Only you can recover yourself from grief by committing to healing. Being new to grief, you may think it's something that descends on you and, at some point, goes away with no action on your part. Healing from heartbreak takes determination, commitment, and intention. Your spirit is stronger than you realize.

If you're not self-aware, you may let the momentous challenges of sudden loss pull you down until you no longer resemble the person you used to be. You could feel continued anger and fear. Despair could consume you, and in turn, you may want to give up on life.

Deep down, you know the people that you miss and love wouldn't want you to quit, but to never give up. They wouldn't want you to be miserable, but to be happy and free. They'd want you to carry on and share the legacy of what you had together. They'd want you to reclaim your life, let go of your sorrow, and experience peace and well-being. This is not to deny the hurt that demands your attention now, but to give you a glimpse of your future as grief softens and love for your beloved grows stronger.

In her book, *You Don't Have to Suffer: A Handbook for Moving Beyond Life's Crises*, Judy Tatelbaum eloquently shares her belief: "It seems to me that the best testimonial we can give to our dead loved ones is how well we recover and live our lives after a loss, not how much we grieve. Our misconception is in imagining that our suffering or how intensely or how long we grieve is a measure of how much we loved. In truth, none of us would want another's grief as a testimonial of their love for us. More likely we would want our loved ones to live healthy, fulfilled lives without us."[viii]

Try this grief healing practice: Imagining Death.
Pretend you died, and your loved ones, children, or friends were left to go on without you. What would you want for them? Would you want them to have their deepest wishes and desires come true? Would you want them to lead fearless, authentic lives? Would you want them to experience joy, love, and freedom?

Would your deceased loved one want these same things for you?

Yes, of course.

It's not too late for you.

There's a purpose for your life.

Your heart will reopen and reawaken.

Great things are still coming, even though you can't see or feel it now.

How can you invite possibility into your life?

Owning Your Grief

"Most people do not know how brave they really are."

—R. E. Chambers

Now that you've considered the possibility of inviting hope and healing into your life, let's focus on sorrow itself. Grief needs your care and attention. In fact, it's necessary to welcome and befriend your sorrow before you can say goodbye and let it go. Sometimes grievers don't want to heal because they mistakenly belief the pain keeps them close to those they lost. In reality, it's the love that keeps you close, not the suffering. You are letting go of the pain and holding onto the love.

All wounds need attention to heal, just as grief does. As a human, of course, you want to avoid pain and suffering. Unfortunately, moving away from your loss prevents you from feeling it, working through it, and integrating it into your being. To feel pain is normal and natural, and it means you are alive. Grief asks you to honor your loss, and in turn, deepens your capacity for compassion, joy, and love.

When I lost Mom, I learned to keep my feelings to myself and was not open. I didn't want to make others uncomfortable, and I had learned to be unexpressive from my mother. When Mom experienced the death of my father, she shared very little with others. She was heartbroken but did not show this pain. Mom never fully resolved her grief. As a child and young adult, I absorbed and felt her sadness, which added another layer of cumulative grief that was necessary for me to heal as an adult.

As I grew older, Mom continued her silence about my father, leaving me with little knowledge of his life, personality, and spirit. Looking back, Mom's intention was to protect me from the pain, but her actions also unintentionally robbed me from knowing my father. Her memories, stories, and experiences of my father were a treasure that I will never know. As a result, his life is a mystery to me.

The way to move toward healing is to complete grief by allowing, experiencing, and expressing it. This includes processing all of your related emotions, whether anger, sadness, guilt, or regret. When you fully express feelings, this allows them to dissolve. Fully experienced grief will disappear, and love will remain. Love will gradually fill the space where suffering currently lives.

Try this daily grief healing practice: Giving Yourself Permission to Express Grief. Allow yourself to honor your profound grief, experience your deep sorrow, and express it in your own way. Give yourself permission to feel exactly how you are feeling and to ignore family patterns, societal expectations, or limiting beliefs about how to handle loss.

Let grief move through you gently with love. Allow your sorrow to surge and subside naturally. If you can, take in small amounts of pain, and then retreat until you're ready to experience the next wave. Do this in whatever process feels right, whether deep breaths, movement, or stillness. Being with and allowing your grief an ideal practice to use during your dedicated time in your healing sanctuary.

How can you express your grief?

Defining Healing

"And once the storm is over, you won't remember how
you made it through, how you managed to survive. You
won't even be sure if the storm is really over. But one thing
is certain. When you come out of the storm, you won't be
the same person who walked in. That's what the storm is
all about."

–Haruki Murakami

Now that you understand the importance of allowing yourself
to express grief, let's consider what healing means to you.
Articulating your definition of healing will strengthen your
ability to recover after sudden loss because you'll have a vision
to work toward.

Consider these questions:

- How would you describe healing?
- What might healing look and feel like to you?
- What will healing mean to you and your family?

Everyone's definition of healing is unique to them and
their experience.

For example, I describe healing as, "thinking of my deceased
loved ones with happiness and not sadness; appreciating the
moments I had with them rather than disparaging the time
I did not; living my life in a way that honors their lives with
joy, meaning, and purpose; and knowing their spirits are
always with me."

A bereaved mother whose teenage son died many years ago
defines healing as, "a constant holding dear to my heart all of

those things I love about him and our time together. Healing is living my new chapter with a willingness to feel my pain and a willingness to let it go as much as I can in my own time. Healing is also discovering the joy that is surely waiting for me in my life as I move forward one step at a time."

A grieving mother whose adult son died suddenly describes healing as, "Peace deep in my heart and soul, connection to my son in everything, engagement with the people I love, purposefulness in my life choices, and contentment with being here now."

Another bereaved mother describes healing as giving herself permission to mourn and say yes to life. She explains, "I say yes to joy. I say yes to loving myself and others. I say yes to gratitude for what I have in my life. I say yes to self-care. I say yes to finding purpose. I say yes to finding my truth and staying true to myself. I say yes to telling my story. I say yes to healing."

To heal, you must *want* to heal. Clients I work with sometimes resist the idea of healing because they believe they will be forgetting their loved one. Nothing can be further from the truth. You can never forget the person who died. It's impossible. You can, however, release the pain and remember the deep love. You can continue to love the deceased while living. You will love the person you lost until you die. And even after you are physically gone, your soul will continue to love.

John W. James and Russell Friedman explain in *The Grief Recovery Handbook: The Action Program for Moving Beyond Death, Divorce, and Other Losses* that "not forgetting" becomes incorrectly entangled with the idea of "not getting over." They further explain, "This crippling idea keeps the griever's heart eternally broken, does not allow for recovery of any kind, and, more often than not, severely limits any fond memories associated with the relationship."[ix]

Try this grief healing practice: Defining Your Healing.
Let's develop your own unique definition of healing. Close your eyes and imagine healing. What do you see? How do you feel? Who is with you? What are you doing? Stay with your vision and notice all the details and sensations. When you are ready, open your eyes.

On the first page of your grief healing journal, write "This is healing_____" and fill in the blank with what you imagined. Review your definition of healing each day and relive the feeling often. When you fully embody your deep desire for healing, you will recover. As time goes on, your definition of healing will change as you grow and transform through loss.

How will you define your healing?

Choosing to Heal with Intention

"Be intentional. Make choices. Take action."

—Judy Brizendine

You didn't have a choice in your loss, but it's your choice how to handle it.

Believe you can heal, and you will.

You can decide how sorrow will affect the rest of your life. You can actively guide your experience and positively influence your path of restoration. Setting an intention to heal will help you achieve your vision of healing. You are setting the course for your desired outcome of your life.

The word intention comes from the Latin root intendere, which means to "stretch toward something." An intention is defined as what you plan to do or achieve, an aim or purpose, or a determination to act in a certain way.

Setting an intention or series of targets will give you a road map to a new way of being, so you can reach the ultimate outcome— to live fully while you're alive despite the devastation of loss.

By intending to become whole again and survive sudden loss, you'll fuel your actions to heal sorrow. You'll begin to gradually believe in the possibility of a renewed future. As William James explains, "Believe that life is worth living, and your belief will help you create the fact."

Making the conscious choice to survive Mom's death was an important restoration tool that I didn't learn until many years after she died. Unfortunately, I let grief passively descend on me, not understanding or knowing that I could consciously choose how to respond to sorrow and manage it with proactive healing practices.

I watched how my mother and mother-in-law, who both lost their husbands, handled heartbreak. I incorrectly learned surviving grief was done passively and not actively. They both lived in quiet sadness with no action on their part to change their internal circumstances. They did not have the necessary support, knowledge, and understanding to know healing was possible and could occur with healthy grieving.

Many years after my parents' deaths when I would miss them, I chose to believe they'd want me to go forward with a joyous, fulfilled life. The conscious choice to cultivate helpful, rather than harmful thoughts supported my well-being at vulnerable times, preventing me from spiraling into deep sadness, where I had been many times before.

Now I acknowledge their physical absence, but revel in their enduring love and spiritual presence. I remember gently, while continuing to love them. I call on their spirits to guide me. My heart is open to their hearts.

Try this daily grief healing practice: Setting Your Intention to Heal. Define your intention to heal through a declarative, meaningful statement, such as, "I am healing" or "I embrace life" or "I have purpose." Choose an intention that feels good to you. Start it in the present tense as if it has already happened. Use words such as "I am" or "I have" or "I embrace" to reinforce *having*, rather than *wanting*, your desired outcome. Use the words "I can" or "I will" to bring attention on what you wish to accomplish. For example, "I can and will recover" is a powerful intention.

State aloud your committed intention and embrace it with your heart and soul. Look into a mirror, deep into your eyes, and repeat your statement as if it had already happened. This important, courageous pronouncement, declared with conviction and believed wholeheartedly, will serve as a life-defining moment to compel your healing and conscious transformation. In addition to this initial, crucial declaration, you'll need to make the intention to heal again and again, day after day, week after week, and year after year to actively mourn and integrate loss into your life.

Now identify one or two important, supportive people in your life, including the person who died, and verbally share your intention with them. Speaking your commitment aloud to others and yourself supports the manifestation of your healing and opens you to receive it. Your mind, body, and spirt responds to your beliefs.

Repeat your intention as often as possible—in the morning, throughout the day, and at bedtime. Feel, know, and sense the deep emotions behind your words. Use a prompt to remember to say your intention throughout the day. For example, when you're getting dressed in the morning, taking a drink of water, or walking by a burning candle, you can repeatedly say "I am healing... I am healing... I am healing..." or the intention you have chosen.

How will you take an active, rather than passive, approach to your healing?

Affirming Your Intention to Heal

"Often the test of courage is not to die but to live."

—Vittorio Alfieri

Now that you have set your intention to heal, you can affirm it. To affirm something means to make firm, state positively, express agreement, or uphold and support. To guide your healing, focus your mind on what you want, and affirm that vision.

You may resist this unfamiliar vision and foreign declaration of your intention to heal. You may not believe it's possible. But the thoughts you tell yourself are often untrue. Over time, these thoughts turn into your beliefs, but they are faulty. The false beliefs reside in your subconscious, so you're not aware of how they affect you. These self-limiting beliefs are detrimental to your recovery if they are not unearthed and evaluated.

The thoughts you think create your emotions, and your reality is created by your emotions. How you are feeling emotionally then determines the action you take or don't take. Think about past situations when you were frustrated, sad, or resigned; recall how you acted when you felt this way. Your outcome likely was not what you wanted because your negative thoughts and untrue beliefs were fueling your emotions, which lead to an undesired result.

In contrast, constructive beliefs support your life. The words you use and the stories you tell yourself have power. They will determine if you will heal. Choose words to bring solace instead of suffering. You can gradually influence your beliefs, and in turn, your reality.

Your task is to uncover faulty beliefs, evaluate them, and choose how to respond.

Try this daily grief healing practice: Transforming Your False Beliefs. To manage your thoughts, notice what you are telling yourself throughout the day. Pay attention to any painful thoughts or beliefs, such as the following:

- It will always be this bad.
- I can't get better.
- Nobody cares about me.
- Next year will be even worse.
- I can't change.

Use these questions to challenge your thoughts and beliefs:

- What am I telling myself right now? (I will never be better.)
- Do you absolutely know this thought is true? (No.)
- How do you act or feel when you believe this thought? (Hopeless and sad.)
- If you couldn't ever feel this thought again, how would you feel? (Hopeful and happy.)
- What is the exact opposite of this thought? (I am getting better.)

When you have a negative thought or false belief, turn it around immediately. Challenge the narrative in your mind and choose thoughts that support healing and recovery from sudden loss. Your mind believes what you tell it, so fill it with encouragement, hope, and renewal. Align your mind with your definition of healing.

Try this daily grief healing practice: Affirming the Opposite. Turn around a false belief in the moment by asking one simple question: "What if the opposite is true?" For example, to respond to the thought, "I will never get better," ask yourself, "What if I can get better?" If your answer lifts your spirits, it affirms your intention to heal.

Next, add the method you will use to make your affirmation occur. For example, consider the statement "I am getting better each day in every way by _____." This can be completed with activities such as attending a weekly grief support meeting, talking to a counselor, calling a friend each Tuesday and Thursday, or learning how to cook or use the lawn mower.

Here are examples to get you started.

False belief: *I will never recover from my loss.*

Positive affirmation: *I am integrating loss into my life. I am courageously facing the unfamiliar. I am growing each day by _____.*

False belief: I will always feel sad.

Positive affirmation: *I am guiding my thoughts. I am doing my best to heal my heart. I am respecting my loved one's life by _____.*

False belief: *I will never be happy again.*

Positive affirmation: *I am honoring my loved one by honoring myself. Every day I do this by _____.*

False belief: *I will always be lost and alone.*

Positive affirmation: *I am using a support system comprised of people who love and care about me. They help me to _____.*

Notice and question what you are telling yourself, especially if it's detrimental to healthy grieving. Use constructive beliefs to influence your life and enhance your healing.

You aren't required to be the same person you were in the past, or even in this moment. You don't have to listen to your thoughts or allow negative emotions to control you. You can get stuck in grief when you try to build your future using the same, painful thoughts, emotions, and experiences, Instead, affirm, imagine, and experience the positive emotions and outcomes you desire in the future.

Shifts in perception will occur when you see and believe in different possibilities for yourself.

What thoughts and beliefs can you challenge?

Allowing Your Painful Emotions

"Many of us spend our whole lives running from feeling with
the mistaken belief that you cannot bear the pain. But you
have already borne the pain. What you have not done is feel
all you are beyond that pain."

—Kahlil Gibran

Now that you understand the importance of affirming your
intention to heal and challenging false beliefs, let's talk about
your emotions. You may be afraid that if you feel all your
painful emotions, the despair will never cease. But nothing
inside of you can make you feel more hurt than you have
already felt. By resisting emotions, your pain will persist
longer than necessary. Instead, when you release sorrow little
by little, the uncomfortable feelings begin to gradually recede
and disappear.

Emotions are energy. This includes both the good and the
bad. I often hear people say that they don't want to feel their
feelings. They want to suppress rather than express feelings.
They falsely believe that when they experience negative
emotions, they are going to fall into a black, bottomless hole
and never return. But when you don't experience your feelings,
you are shutting off your own energy, which is your life force.
When you close this power source, you will miss future joy.

Feeling equates to healing. Remember, all feelings want to be
felt. They come up to be felt, so feel them. That is their sole
purpose. Emotions want to be in motion. Once you express
your emotions, they will transform and dissipate.

Consider these questions:

How can I respect my emotions?

How can I allow my feelings to naturally move through me?

How can I trust and surrender to healing?

You're likely not used to noticing in an expressive, non-judgmental way what's occurring for you. Whatever you're feeling right now is okay. All emotions and feelings are acceptable, even the ones you think aren't. Practice being with your emotions using love, compassion, and gentleness.

How can you honor your feelings?

Soothing Resistance to Grieving

"No one ever told me that grief felt so like fear."

−C. S. Lewis

You may experience resistance to healing grief, even though you want to feel better. Avoiding the prospect of facing intense pain and upsetting emotions is normal. Instead, reframe the experience by acknowledging your apprehension as well as your power to choose your response.

Most people think that surrendering to unwanted feelings means losing control. The unpredictability of emotions and changed moods can be frustrating, embarrassing, and inconvenient. You may want to lock down the emotions and keep them in check. But the feelings are still in you and have nowhere to go.

Instead of trying to fight them, let the feelings flow through you and release everything. Be present to the pain when it occurs so you can fully express the related feelings. Notice and allow each of your emotions as they occur. Live your experience as it's happening in the moment rather than distracting yourself or running away from your fear.

Try this daily grief healing practice: Facing Your Fears. To proactively address your fears, make a list of everything that frightens or upsets you. Spend some quiet time asking yourself what you're afraid of. Take three to five minutes and jot down your responses in your grief healing journal. Do it quickly, keep your pen flowing, and do not censor what you are writing. You may be surprised by what shows up.

For example, your list might include:

- Losing control and not being able to regain it
- Crying so much I cannot stop
- Feeling overwhelmed and afraid
- Expressing anger at a higher power
- Feeling guilt and regret that I could have done more

If your answers feel forced, try writing with your non-dominant hand, which will help stimulate your inner thoughts. Alternately, when you go to bed, ask for what you need to know. This will activate your subconscious mind to provide answers. Record these insights as you receive them. Once you identify the fears that block healing, you can then determine ways to alleviate them.

The next question to ask is: "When I feel fear, anxiety, or worry, how can I alleviate the feeling?" In two minutes, brainstorm all the small actions you could take. Next to each fear in your journal, write an idea to lessen it. Add additional ways to relieve your fears as you think of them.

You may want to call a friend to discuss your concern, learn more information, make an appointment with a professional, read affirmations to soothe yourself, go for a walk to clear your head, listen to music to relax, write in your journal to release troubling thoughts, or take a nap. When a fearful moment strikes, refer to your grief healing journal for ideas to calm yourself.

Do what you can, right where you are, to soothe yourself. You will begin to move through your distress by taking small actions each day. These concrete, doable actions are how you move toward healing.

How can you soothe your fears?

Letting Go of Emotions

"Whatever arises, love that."

—Matt Kahn

Stuck emotions and painful feelings will affect your thinking, the choices that you make, and your future joy. These trapped emotions can block you from giving and receiving love freely.

People sometimes get stuck in grief because they only partially experience their feelings. When you hold in grief and don't let it go, you cannot complete the experience. You need to work on actively releasing painful emotions. According to Dr. Bradley Nelson, the author of *The Emotion Code*, emotionally-charged events from your past can affect you in the form of "trapped emotions," which is emotional energy that lives in your body.[x] These emotions can cause and create pain, distress, and even disease. You've likely recognized other grievers by their expressions, slow movements, or physical distress.

For any emotion you don't like or want, your instinctive response is to stop the feeling. But whenever you cut off your emotions, you also cut off love. When you shut down, it means there's an emotion that you are afraid of feeling. The key is to welcome all emotions, even those that are the most uncomfortable.

Try this daily grief healing practice: Processing Emotions to Reach Peace. Use this method to release and remove trapped emotions. This process is a Pure Awareness Technique™ and is from the work of Inner Greatness Global founder and author Tom Stone, who I trained with to learn energy healing.

To begin the step-by-step process to achieve peace:

1. Feel the sensation of the emotion. Notice where the energy of grief is in your physical body. Ask yourself to complete this sentence: "When I think about the sudden death of the person I care about, I feel_____." Then ask yourself, "Where do I physically feel this emotion in my body?" Perhaps you sense a pain, knot, or constriction in your stomach, chest, or throat. It may feel like angst, uneasiness, or butterflies.

2. Rate the intensity of the physical pain on a scale of zero to ten with ten being the strongest and zero being no pain.

3. Identify where the sensation is the strongest in your physical body. Find the most intense part or center of this energy and focus your attention there.

4. Allow the sensation to be in your body without trying to change, solve, or push it away. Ignore the temptation to think about what is happening, Instead, keep your mind quiet and simply notice the strongest part of the feeling in your body. Be present to the energy of the emotion.

5. Observe the changing sensation. It may become stronger, less intense, stay the same, or seem to move. Continue to focus on the most intense part of the sensation, by noticing, allowing, and witnessing the feeling.

6. Consciously stay with the feeling. Your body is experiencing this emotion and releasing the stored energy. Keep simply noticing the sensation until the feeling subsides and the intensity of the emotion reduces to zero on the pain scale. The release can happen quickly or take many minutes.

7. Continue to feel what's happening in your body until there's nothing left but a sense of neutrality or peace. If you stop before you reach completion, the emotion has not been fully released. The key is to continue the process until you no longer have awareness of the physical feeling. To successfully complete the experience, simply keep noticing what remains until there's nothing left to feel.

Whenever a new overwhelming feeling emerges, use this process to release it. Because energy can be stored in your body for a prolonged time, you may need to use this Pure Awareness Technique™ often to release new and old feelings. When you experience uneasiness, stress, fear, or any unpleasant emotion, ask yourself where you feel the sensation in your body, and then begin the process to restore neutrality.

Tom Stone specifically calls the technique described above the IN Technique™. He created a free phone app with which you can guide yourself through the IN Technique™ and other Pure Awareness Techniques™ with interactive audio instructions to use at your own pace.

I introduce the process to all my clients because it is the easiest, most effective way to bring peace. If you are hesitant to try any practices in this book, use this one first. You'll receive the most noticeable results, and this may inspire you to use more of the healing exercises.

This process is ideal to use in your healing sanctuary. Each time you use your safe space to grieve, you can access your innate abilities to heal and change emotions. The gift of opening yourself to your feelings is that, in time, they'll dissolve, and you'll be free of them.

What emotions, feelings, or fears would you like to release right now?

Identifying Cumulative Grief

"Opening to the little losses will make room for the bigger
ones when they come along."

–Alexandra Kennedy

In addition to your current loss, you may have experienced
many hurts over your life. In your youth, you may have endured
the losses of friends, pets, homes, and family. As you got older,
you may have suffered the loss of relationships, health, dreams,
careers, or security. These accumulated losses can be unfelt
or unacknowledged.

Your past hurts cause a backlog of unprocessed feelings.
This cumulative grief from unresolved losses can make you
unknowingly turn away from life, others, or yourself. This
buried sorrow can erupt unexpectedly or be triggered by
another loss. "Unresolved grief can show up in such symptoms
as chronic physical ailments, fearfulness, depression,
overworking, addiction, social isolation or addiction," says
Alexandra Kennedy, therapist and author of *Honoring Grief*.[xi]
The pain you feel may be overbearing, yet familiar. The feelings
you have now can be magnified or intensified by lingering,
cumulative grief.

Try this grief healing practice: Identifying Life Losses.
Reflect on the losses you have experienced in your life up to
now. The exercise should take only a few minutes.

In your grief healing journal, create a timeline from your birth
to present day and note *all* of your significant losses. Include
your related feelings and age at time of loss. List *any* type of
loss, such as friends, pets, homes, health, relationships, jobs,

money, or status. The losses may seem small in comparison to what you are going through now.

Pay attention to how you worked through past situations. Note the healthy and unhealthy ways in which you dealt with your grief. Determine if any patterns emerged that will help you to cope with sorrow now.

When I did this exercise, I found unexpressed grief and feelings due to many things including the death of my father (age four—I felt sad, confused, and alone), a new school and different home in an unfamiliar city (age eight—I felt scared, powerless, and unsupported), loss of friends (age twelve—I felt betrayed, vulnerable, and ashamed), first painful breakup (age fourteen—I felt heartbroken, embarrassed, and rejected), loss of financial stability (age sixteen—I felt afraid, uncertain, and insecure), and workplace bullying (age twenty—I felt angry, berated, and attacked).

Now, most importantly, review your timeline and identify any losses that weren't processed that can be grieved now. For example, I remembered the painful change of moving that occurred when I was eight years old that wasn't fully acknowledged. I had to grieve this hidden pain from long ago, just like you may need to let go of old hurts now.

Many people have unexpressed loss from past experiences as well as generational grief that was passed on from parents to children. When you acknowledge that unresolved sorrow exists, it can move through you to be released. Honor and love *all* of your losses to facilitate healing.

Use your healing sanctuary to grieve the buried hurts you identified. To notice your progress, compare how you feel before and after spending time in your safe space each day.

What cumulative losses do you need to let go of?

Practice Three

Renew: Foster a Support System

Caring for Your Self

"Don't just be good to others. Be good to yourself, too."

—Unknown

The grief you are experiencing now is something you likely have never encountered previously. This is foreign territory, and you'll need support to help you successfully navigate this new terrain. Comfort and understanding are necessary to your survival right now. A support system that understands your unique emotional needs is essential for renewal and restoration.

Building a support system may be new to you. And that's okay because this chapter will help you cultivate ways to honor, support, and renew yourself as you begin to rebuild your life.

You can define what integrating loss into your life will look and feel like for you. You can decide what you need and want for you. Who best to do this, but you?

You are the master of your grief journey.

You are the expert of your experience.

You are the teacher to those who don't understand.

Let family and friends know your grief healing is a priority. This means educating others on how they can help you to adjust, accept, and absorb this major change in your life. Ignore any judgmental responses or inaccurate interpretations of your experience. Take the opportunity to educate others on what you need to heal. Others will need your direction and guidance to best support you.

In addition to the help of others, you can provide a support system for yourself through self-care. To care for yourself means to serve as advocate for your healing and renewal. What you want and need matters—especially now, when exploring the unfamiliar world of grief.

Self-care means providing loving acts of kindness to yourself even when you don't feel like it or when you think it is foolish. Self-care means taking care of your mental, emotional, physical, and spiritual health with deliberate action. Self-care means to renew yourself by knowing and fulfilling your needs. When you take care of yourself first, then you will have more capacity to take care of others.

Prior to your loss, perhaps you stood in the background and assisted others and asked nothing for yourself. Maybe you were the person who got things done, who did everything for everyone else, or who didn't lean on others. Perhaps you didn't practice self-care or take care of your needs first.

Now, you may be experiencing emotional outbursts or have days where you don't want to speak, walk, or move. You may crave isolation, wanting to stay home and avoid others. You may not yet know what you need or want to feel better. If you haven't received support and nurturing in the past, you may not realize it's something you require now.

When my father died suddenly in the early 1970s, I was a young child who was only four years old. As a new widow, Mom, who was a homemaker, had to suddenly take over her husband's large business. This was especially unusual to have a woman running a company during this time period, when the societal norm was for women to stay home to care for their families. Mom didn't have anywhere to turn for expert business support or help to raise me. Her parents were deceased, and she was an

only child. Mom buried her needs and sadness. She appeared
to "act strong" and "move on." She didn't know how to build a
viable support system or use self-care.

When I was new to loss, I repeated this family pattern. I
wasn't used to people helping me. I didn't have a solid support
structure and was operating under the conditioned response
that uncomfortable feelings were not talked about, and it was
better to pretend you were fine.

I was previously the "go-to" person for others, and I prided
myself on efficiently getting things done at work and at home.
Now, I couldn't do the same amount of activity I had done in
the past. I didn't know how to ask for help. Instead, I put up a
"brave front" for others to prevent their discomfort and to hide
my shame for not being able to "move on" because I thought
that was what I was "supposed" to do.

To combat the pressure from both yourself and from others,
you may appear to feel better. But you may also know this is
a lie—when you're putting on a front for others, especially.
Instead, ask yourself what you really want. Listen closely to the
answers. You do have a choice in how you react and what you
do. You'll begin to naturally direct your healing. You'll hear the
needed insights come from deep within your soul. Trust your
internal guidance system to nurture yourself.

You'll likely hear messages like these:

- It's time to make your needs a priority.
- It's time to treat yourself with extreme care.
- It's time to focus on yourself.
- Your loss has turned your life upside down. Now, more
  than ever, loving and paying attention to yourself
  is critical.

To engage in your renewal:

- Listen to and follow your inner being.
- Pay attention to what you require moment by moment.
- Rest and don't push yourself.

In grief and daily life, there are a lot of "shoulds" and "musts" imposed by yourself and others. You may have likely heard the expression to not "should" all over yourself.

The word "should" often carries feelings of shame and guilt with it. It's often an internal way to beat yourself up for not meeting the unrealistic, demanding expectations you impose on yourself. These rigid standards were likely internalized and programmed from what you learned growing up.

Try this daily self-care practice: Examining Your Shoulds. When you tell yourself that you should or must do something, stop and examine your thought. Then, ask yourself, "Whose standard is this?" or "Whose instruction book am I following?" Then, ask yourself what you really want to do. It will likely be something different. For example, you might think, "I should write a thank you note, but I really want to take a nap."

To counteract your "should" statements, substitute the word "could." The idea that you "could" do something is more liberating and implies you have a choice. This cultivates self-kindness because you are using a loving, forgiving tone in your self-talk.

To help you know what you really need or want, finish this statement, "If I loved myself, I would_____." Act on the answer you receive. For example, if you want to take a nap, take a nap. If you can't do exactly what you need in the current moment, do something close. For example, stop and rest in a chair if a nap is not feasible.

Give yourself gentle, loving care whenever you can. To make it a habit, post this statement, "If I loved myself, I would_____," on your mobile phone, date book, bathroom mirror, car dashboard, or wherever you'll easily see it. This visual reminder will support the important act of caring for yourself.

Try this daily self-care practice: Switching Up Your Self-Talk. Act as an inner caring friend to yourself by talking to yourself as you would converse with your best friend. You'd likely offer encouragement, inspiration, and good advice.

Observe your self-talk throughout the day. Notice if you are judgmental and harsh or gentle and loving. Begin to replace any negative self-talk and inner criticism with nurturing and caring statements, such as:

I am sorry you had a bad day. Tomorrow will be better, so let's rest right now.

I am sorry others think you should be feeling better by now. Let's give you all the time, rest, and care you need.

I am sorry that someone hurt your feelings. It's okay to feel sad. Others may not understand what you're going through. Let's do our best to surround you with supportive people.

Draw a line down the middle of a piece of paper in your grief healing journal. On the left side, note any negative statements you mentally repeat to yourself during the day. On the right side, write reassuring, encouraging statements to use instead. The goal is to learn how to provide self-soothing affirmations to nourish your wounded heart.

How can you begin to care for yourself more?

Reaching Out for Help

"Joy shared is doubled, and grief shared is halved."

—*The Sunday Magazine*

Now that you are beginning to understand the importance of caring for yourself, it's time to consider how you can start to accept support from others. Unfortunately, you may be so depleted that it can feel impossible to ask for assistance. You may be afraid to lean on others if you haven't done so in the past. It may feel uncomfortable to accept help now.

About six months after Mom died, I weighed a meek 110 pounds due to sudden weight loss. I suffered migraine headaches, endured the care of a neurologist, and experienced an excessive need to sleep. I was physically sick with grief—something I didn't even know could happen. Despite these conditions, I appeared "fine" on the outside. Perhaps it was wishful thinking from others combined with my failure to ask for assistance as well as my false façade. Inside, I knew differently. I felt like a part of me was lost. I was bewildered, disoriented, and was not functioning effectively.

I wanted to talk about my mother but thought others didn't want to listen. I wanted to say her name but believed others didn't want to hear it. I wanted to cry but imagined others didn't want to see it. These limiting beliefs appeared true because I had not yet learned to express my needs.

Many people think they must control their mourning to be strong for others. You may have learned to keep your needs to yourself, as I did. You may think that it's gracious to thwart others' requests to provide love, compassion, or support.

But that is not helpful for your healing. Everyone, including you, needs a chance to grieve and mourn loss. Those who care about you and understand grief won't think less of you for showing your emotions.

Others may want you to feel better and tell you how good you are doing. To appease them, you may try to act and look normal, but inside you know the truth. Being strong and hiding your grief only makes it harder on you. As you learned in Chapter Two, to get out of pain, you must go through it. Covering up sorrow does not work.

Let's reframe this mode of "I can do it alone" thinking. Instead, consider the following:

It's good to be taken care of by compassionate, nurturing people who want to support you. It's okay to receive help...and lots of it. It's safe to take advantage of the comfort offered.

Tell others the truth about how you are feeling.

Be vulnerable and let yourself depend on someone.

Open yourself to give and receive love.

I let a good friend accompany me to the cemetery when she offered, even though I thought it was a "bother." It wasn't a nuisance to her but a chance to genuinely support me when she wasn't sure how. Now, I fondly recall my friend bringing a single-stemmed red rose on a snowy day to place on my mother's grave on the anniversary of Mom's death. That act made me feel seen and heard. My loss was acknowledged, and I felt loved.

Allow people to tend to your well-being, although it may seem uncomfortable. Permit others to serve you now, just as you would help them in their time of need. Ask for support.

How can you reach out for support?

Asking for Specific Help

"He that conceals his grief finds no remedy for it."

–Turkish Proverb

Others want to help, but they often aren't sure what to do. Help them help you. They will respond to guidance or direct requests from you when you're specific. Remember, many people have not experienced the death of someone they care about, so they don't naturally know how to assist you.

Close your eyes, and ask, "What do I need at this moment?" Do you want emotional care, financial support, or household help? Do you want companionship, time away from home, or a break from your job?

If you have difficulty composing a list, enlist a trusted confidant, friend, or family member to help develop it. To get started, you might say, "People want to support me, but I am not sure where to start. Can you help me write a 'how to assist me' list?"

Together you can brainstorm ideas. For example, you could use a list like this:

1.   Daily Chores: Wash laundry, cut the grass, clean the house, return phone calls, or run errands.

2. Meals: Shop for groceries, pack lunches, plan and
    prepare food, or drop off meals.

3. Children: Provide transportation to school or daycare,
    help with homework, drive kids to activities and sporting
    events, or spend time with younger children.

4. Social Activities: Accompany me to activities, see a
    movie, go out for coffee or lunch, see a sporting event, or
    serve as company when I need it.

5. House Repairs: Install new or additional locks, repair
    broken items, mount seasonal storm windows, trim trees
    or bushes, paint, or pack boxes.

6. Car Maintenance: Change oil, fill or rotate tires, replace
    battery, or provide advice in purchasing or selling a car.

After you've identified your priorities, consider who can
support you, and compare these people's strengths to the tasks.
A brother may be helpful with car maintenance, a neighbor
may be glad to assist with house repairs, a mother may be
supportive with daily chores, and a work colleague may be
useful for companionship.

Ask a friend or family member to share your requests for
assistance if you are uncomfortable in doing so or don't have
enough energy. The clearer you are in requests, the more likely
your needs will be met.

You are worthy and deserving of others' care. Don't go it alone;
extra assistance will help you through grief, especially in the
beginning. Now is the time to seek support.

If you still feel uneasy, start small. Notice minor ways others
can assist. Practice receiving care by making a simple request
such as, "Can you help me carry these boxes to the curb?"
or "Can I accept your offer for lunch today?" By asking for

what you need when you need it, you'll continue to build
your confidence.

Try this daily self-care practice: Accepting Assistance.
At the end of the day, reflect upon the opportunities you
had for assistance. How did you feel? How did you respond?
If you weren't comfortable receiving support, how can you
act differently in the future? For example, instead of shying
away from kindness, perhaps you could say "Yes, I'll take
you up on your offer" or "Thank you" or "I appreciate your
thoughtfulness." The next time you want to pass up another's
offer of assistance, reconsider the gift.

What do you need most from others right now?

Finding Support from the Right People

"If you can't be yourself when you're with people, don't
change yourself. Change the people."

—Cheryl Richardson

Now that you have identified where you need help, be sure
to find the right people to assist you. Some won't be able to
encourage you because of their discomfort and uneasiness.
Many people are fearful of death or have anxiety about their
own mortality or loss of family members. Most people simply
haven't been taught how to talk about loss, cope with sorrow, or
work through grief.

You may find your group of companions is rearranged after
death. You may lose touch with close friends who don't call or
seem apprehensive. You'll be surprised by those who show up

to assist and disappointed by those who don't. It's likely most people do care, but they just don't know how to show it.

My longtime close friends didn't attend Mom's funeral, which was only a few days before Christmas. They thought it was too much driving to make two long trips, one for the funeral and one for the holidays, especially when their first child was due in a few weeks. Of course, this all made logical sense, but I felt hurt and deserted when I needed them. After that, our previously important friendship faded away because I didn't make any attempt to stay in contact, nor did they.

Like me, you may realize that before the sudden death of your beloved person, you didn't know how to support a grieving person effectively. Perhaps you can give a little slack to those you still want in your life who don't say and do the right things. Perhaps you'll have compassion to forgive the people who weren't available for you in the way you wanted. Perhaps you'll be able to help others when loss hits their lives.

There are others who can and will naturally comfort you. They'll want to nurture, love, and cheer you on. Those who have gone through something similar will empathize with your daily challenges and acknowledge your pain. Although they don't know exactly how you feel, they've been there in their own way.

You may find you are drawn to those who've had similar experiences. As you become more familiar with grief healing, you may want to assist others who are newer to death. Your experience and outlook will bond you to different people, and you'll make new friendships.

About eleven years after Mom's death, I became closer to a couple who had lost their one-year-old daughter, Noel. My son, Jacob, was only six months older than her. I could relate to their tragedy as a parent myself, even though I could never fully understand. I could freely talk to my friends about Noel when many people could not, especially parents of young children. Although we had different types of grief, the commonality of losing loved ones deepened our friendship.

Now is the time to surround yourself with caring and compassionate people who can listen, encourage, and guide you. Spend time with others you feel good around—those who lift your energy or give you a shoulder to cry on. Talk to people who understand—those who listen to your honest feelings with openness.

In turn, consider limiting your interactions with toxic people— those who aren't sensitive to your needs, who drain your energy, and take away your personal power. If others are telling you how you should feel or not feel, they aren't the correct people to serve as grief companions.

Let's examine your support system to ensure you spend time with the right people, those who treat you with respect, empathy, and reverence.

1. List the names of the ten people with whom you have the most important relationships.

2. Give yourself one hundred points. Now allocate these one hundred points to the ten people identified in step one above, assigning points in relation to the care and positive energy you receive from them. For instance, person number one may receive fifteen points, person number two may receive twenty-five points, person number three may receive two points, and so on.

3. You'll probably discover that most of your useful support comes from just one or two of the ten people. Who are these individuals? Write them down on a separate list.

4. Give yourself another one hundred points to allocate to these same ten people. Allocate points to each person in relation to how much time you spend with each of them. You'll likely realize you are spending more time with unsupportive individuals who are negative influences. Who are these individuals?

5. Review and compare your results. Are you spending more time with less supportive people?

6. Answer these questions: "How can I spend more time with the people who are the best at helping and comforting me?" and "Who should I spend less time with?"

You know your heart. You know who is the most capable of helping you. You know the pace of healing that is correct for you. Remember, a good support network simply stands by your side to provide encouragement, understanding, and compassion.

Who are the right people to support you?

Talking about Sorrow

"Give sorrow words."

—William Shakespeare

Now that you have identified compassionate, caring people who can support you, determine who you can easily and comfortably talk with to share your feelings.

After the funeral, when you need comfort the most, many people stop conversing about your loved one. When Mom died,

I couldn't believe that the rest of the world kept going and returned to daily life when I had been shaken to the core. The work of grieving was just starting, and I couldn't have been more unprepared. I needed someone to talk too.

You'll need others to listen as you express your emotions, whether you're experiencing hopelessness, disbelief, or despair. Empathetic, kind-hearted companions can make you feel understood, acknowledged, and honored as they let you speak freely from your heart without judgment or criticism.

After Mom's death, many people were uneasy with me, including my husband. But one of my friends was very open with her feelings. She prompted responses from me with thoughtful questions and encouragement. She was my lifeline at the time, and everyone needs at least one person to serve in this role.

For those who haven't experienced the death of a beloved person, they may think they are being respectful by not talking about your loss. They may mistakenly believe grief is over in a month or a year and not understand the lifelong impact. They may not want to upset you more, so they remain quiet.

A client whose husband died said when she would get together with her friends, it was like there was a "big elephant" in the room. Some of them had no idea what to say to her and were very uncomfortable. She finally just said, "Please don't be uneasy. I would love to talk about my husband. It really helps."

Give yourself and others the opportunities to speak and share. Initiate the discussion using the name of your loved one. Ask questions, such as "What do you remember the most about_____?" or "What's your favorite memory

about_____?" What was he like at work? At church?
At family gatherings? At parties?

At first, it may seem too painful or uncomfortable. The
discomfort will no doubt lessen the more you talk. As you start
more conversations, others will know that it is okay, and they
may be more at ease going forward.

My mother-in-law, LaVon, lost her mom, Tina, over seventy
years ago when LaVon was only nine years old. LaVon, who
acts as a surrogate mother to me, sends me beautiful flowers on
the anniversary of Mom's death each year. Most importantly,
she welcomes the conversation about how I am feeling. LaVon
remembers the significance of her own mother, and I receive an
understanding companion. By accepting her help, not only am I
supporting myself, but also offering solace to her.

Seek out trusted confidants who allow you to talk as much and
as often as you need to about your situation, the person you
miss, and your memories. Engage with those who respect your
sorrow and offer hope. Talk about the story of the deceased if it
feels right to you. For example, you can discuss:

- What happened?
- Where were you?
- How did you find out?
- What emotions did you feel?
- What did you think?

Reviewing the death helps you accept the reality of the situation
and acknowledges your sudden loss. Tell your story over and
over if you like. Talk about what happened in the past, what
is happening now, and what you would like to happen in
the future.

You may have family members who choose not to talk about your loved one—that is okay. It's unlikely they don't miss the person who died. Instead, they may miss the deceased so much that just thinking about the beloved person can hurt too much. If at times you don't feel like talking, you also have the right to be silent.

Who can you openly talk to?

Putting Your Needs First

and Expressing Preferences

"I have come to believe that caring for myself is not self-indulgent. Caring for myself is an act of survival."

—Audre Lorde

Now that you've identified the right people to talk to, it's time to ask for the necessary support and to make your needs a priority. Lean on the caring support system you have identified—the people who are both willing and able to help, honor your preferences, and meet your needs with love and respect.

When you reach out to others, the burden of coping with unexpected death can be lessened. Seeking help should not be considered a "crutch," but instead an important lifeline.

I was asked to do a presentation for colleagues on a new work process shortly after Mom died. I was afraid to ask someone else to take it over for me because I didn't want to "look bad" or appear incapable. Instead of acting on my inner knowing that the presentation would be too much to handle, I plodded forward and stressed myself out for almost two weeks. I tried to rise to the occasion, but, about a day before the speech, I finally asked my supervisor to have someone else present the information. I could have prevented my unnecessary tension by asking for help when I knew I needed it.

So don't wait.

Seek support when you need it.

Tap into the people, activities, and thoughts that steer you in the right direction.

When you are challenged, share your intentions to feel better.

Allow trusted friends to alert you when they see you veering off course. Consider these suggestions when you feel pressured to act before you are ready:

1. Express preferences. Pay attention to your inclinations. Let others know what you can't or don't want to do. It's not necessary to explain, defend, or debate your decision.

2. Know your limits. If you are tired or don't feel like doing something, you can choose not to do it. Your friends and family will understand if you don't join in some activities.

3. Say no. If you are invited out, but may not feel like going, it's okay to say no. Others may want to take your mind from the situation. If you choose to decline some activities, you don't need to give a reason.

A week after Mom's death, my husband, Bill, insisted I go to a family wedding with him. He thought being active and interacting with others would make me feel better. Bill was doing his best to help me with what he knew about grief at the time.

I unfortunately "went along" to avoid conflict and honor his needs instead of my own. I was miserable at the wedding. I had to watch the video presentation of the "happy times" of the newlyweds' life and unsuccessfully force back tears at their joyous occasion. It was too soon for me to be out in public. I knew this before I attended but didn't set a boundary and say "no" to my well-meaning husband.

The concept of "healthy selfishness" is explained by author Katherine Woodward Thomas in her book, Calling in *"The*

One," as knowing your limits and setting them. She says, "It means you prioritize self-care over caring for others. It insists that you communicate your feelings, even when your feelings are inconvenient to others. It includes the ability to rest when tired and to ask for what you want and need, when you want and need it."[xii]

Try this daily self-care practice: Using Boundaries.
If you aren't familiar with setting boundaries or limits with others, plan on giving yourself time to respond to requests. Rather than answering quickly, you can say, "I'll need to review my schedule," or "I need to check with _____," or "Let me think about it."

Next, ask yourself, "Is this request something I'd really like to do or am I agreeing due to obligation or guilt?" It's important to think about your needs first rather than worrying about how others may respond.

If you choose to decline the request, do so with decisiveness and honesty. You can say, "I'd like a rain check for another time," or "I'll have to pass this time, but look forward to seeing you in the future," or "I already have too many things going on this week, so I can't attend." Remember, it's not your responsibility to manage others' reactions or make them feel better. Instead, gauge your success on how you feel by making the best choice for you.

How can you put your needs first?

Being an Advocate for Your Needs

and Emotions

"Speak your mind even if your voice shakes."

—Maggie Kuhn

As you learn to express your preferences and put your wishes first, you'll be serving as an advocate for yourself. Continue to be open with your support system about your needs and wants.

You will experience many emotional ups and downs when grieving. Your feelings, energy, and interests can change quickly and dramatically with little warning. This can be startling to both yourself and others, and you'll need to educate others on how to help you.

You'll think you are doing better, but then, out of nowhere, bursts of sorrow appear. You may wonder how you can feel good one moment and terrible the next. These grief attacks are normal and can occur six days, six months, or six years from your beloved's death. They don't mean you are going backward in your healing. Rest assured, you're not losing the progress you've made; instead, you're oscillating between grieving and healing while gradually moving forward.

"Grief is characterized by periods of intense distress and relative calm that can be referred to as acute and subtle grief," according to Sameet M. Kumar, who is the author of *Grieving Mindfully*. Kumar describes acute grief as the only thing you can attend to because it demands all of your attention. In contrast, subtle grief allows you to work and carry on with your life in periods of calm, while still grieving. Some of your feelings may linger under the surface, waiting for an opportunity to present themselves.[xiii]

Because you will move between acute and subtle grief, your healing process can be unpredictable and will not follow stages or a straight line, as you learned in Chapter One. Instead, grief is more like an upward, unending spiral, similar to a Slinky, which you may have played with as a child. With each twist, which represents the ups and downs of grief, you are moving up the spring. Each turn gets less painful, perhaps leaving you feeling better than before, but at times returning you to acute grief. You're making gradual progress as you move up the spiral, spending less time in acute grief.

Grief's intensity will change. Anything that reminds you of your loss can trigger a grief reaction, even seemingly minor or random things. Events, places, people, music, scents, or images can trigger strong grief feelings. An anniversary, holiday, birthday, or special occasion can prompt fresh sorrow.

Perhaps your tears start by observing a romantic couple at a restaurant, overhearing a parent and young child laughing, or seeing a mother and son spending time together. Perhaps your grief is triggered by grocery shopping for one less person, seeing an empty chair at the table, or noticing a vacant garage stall. Perhaps your sadness is triggered from driving by a favorite place, talking to certain people, or doing an activity.

One of my favorite activities to do with Mom was shopping. After her death, when I saw a mother and daughter together at a store talking about everyday things, I felt a sharp sting of sadness. I opened a retail gift store about four years after Mom died, and I would get those familiar twinges of pain when a parent and child came in the shop together. I longed for those everyday moments with my mother that I had taken for granted.

A bereaved mother who was a client felt intense anguish and sadness when she received high school graduation invitations from her deceased son's friends. Her precious son had died twelve months earlier and would not be graduating with his class. Another grieving parent said her pain was indescribable when she received a wedding invitation from her deceased daughter's fiancé who had fallen in love again and was getting married to another woman.

Educate your personal circle about your right to experience eruptions of grief in public or private. Because others who aren't experiencing profound sorrow have an easier time predicting their feelings, they may not understand or wonder why your moods change dramatically.

Let your friends and family know surges of emotion will happen. Explain how they can support you, whether that means letting you cry, talk, rest, or be alone.

I have never gone to the cemetery without crying, and it has been over twenty years since Mom's death. My husband expects this and simply gives me a hug and a kiss. Now, my son accompanies us to the cemetery and sees me cry. He is learning that it's okay and necessary to express painful feelings and show your emotions.

Continue to expect yourself to go through a wave of emotions with the sudden flashes of pain growing further apart. Each expressed feeling gets you closer to integrating loss into your being. You will feel gradual renewal and growth as you go through the transformational process of healing grief.

What triggers your grief? How can you educate others to support you?

Exploring and Breaking Grief Myths

"Though you should reach out to others as you do the work of mourning, you should not feel obligated to accept the unhelpful responses you may receive from some people. You are the one who is grieving, and, as such, you have certain 'rights' no one should try to take away from you."

–Dr. Alan Wolfelt

Another critical component of self-care is accepting beliefs that work for you and rejecting those that do not. There are a lot of myths, misconceptions, and inaccurate information about healing from unexpected loss that continue to be perpetuated in our society. Unfortunately, those supporting you may have bought into these misconceptions because of the lack of familiarity and firsthand experience with death, dying, and grieving.

As you integrate loss into your life, do not believe these unhelpful messages. Be aware of the myths of how to cope with grief, and counteract them with empowering beliefs on how to heal sorrow.

Common myths include the following:

- Getting back to your old, normal self is possible.
- Grieving ends at a specific time.
- Following the five stages of grief is the right way.
- Keeping busy will eliminate or lessen grief.
- Being strong is best.
- Crying or getting help shows weakness.

If you begin to accept these messages as true, you may think you should act differently rather than following your natural, authentic path to healing. You may feel unnecessary shame, guilt, and doubt about your actions.

Instead, act as a guide for others who support you. Act as an advocate for yourself as you learn what brings you peace and healing. Act as an inspiration for others to follow their hearts and express their grief authentically.

What unhelpful information have you encountered about grief?

Dealing with Misinformation

"When you really listen to yourself, you can heal yourself."

–Ceanne Derohan

With the misinformation and misunderstandings about how to heal grief, sometimes people will say things that may anger or upset you. In contrast, others may be very supportive and understand what you are going through. Your task is to distinguish supportive statements from the unsupportive.

Disregard any unhelpful replies immediately, and concentrate on beneficial comments and resulting empowering thoughts. For those statements you may not like, simply say, "Thank you for your concern," to end the conversation. Alternately, to gently educate the person on your needs, say, "That doesn't help me," or "That is true, but not helpful."

To illustrate, someone may say, "He lived a long life." Yes, that is a "true" statement, but it's not a "helpful" statement. Of course, the grieving person wanted his or her loved one to live even longer.

Here are things others should *not* say, but that you'll likely hear:

- "I know how you feel."
- "I understand how hard your loss must be for you and your children."
- "Let me tell you how my friend handled a similar time."

Others should avoid comparisons. No one understands your distinctive grief.

- "You are young, you can remarry."
- "Be glad you have two other healthy children."
- "You can still have another child."

Others need to understand there is no replacement for the person who died. The physical presence of your loved one is unique and irreplaceable.

- "Time heals everything."
- "Keep your chin up."
- "You will never be given more than you can handle."

Others should avoid clichés, because they do not accurately reflect the length, depth, and intensity of your mourning.

- "At least you can travel now that you aren't caring for him anymore."
- "At least he didn't suffer."
- "At least you didn't have any children."

Others should avoid statements that begin with "At least..." These statements do not acknowledge your despair and personal anguish.

- "Everything happens for a reason."
- "He's in a better place."
- "It was God's will."

Others should not assume a death is for the best or in any way a blessing. You would've liked your beloved to be alive and with you.

- "He lived a long, full life."
- "At least she's not in pain anymore."
- "Be thankful you had him for so long."

Others should not comment on the health or length of your beloved's life. Most people think the time with their loved one is never enough.

- "The death of a child is the worst type of loss."
- "You have lost only one family member."
- "The death of a spouse is more difficult than the loss of a parent."

Others should not compare types of loss. These needless judgments minimize your individual grief.

You get to explore how you think and feel right now and do not have to follow how others expect you to act or respond. If possible, try to listen to the love behind the words of others. Others can be well meaning, but their words may fail them because they simply do not know what to say.

Try this self-care practice: Preplanning Your Replies. Consider preparing and planning your responses to unhelpful comments. Although this task may be difficult, it will help you cope better when you may be caught off guard by another's actions or comments. Draw a line down the center of a piece of paper in your grief healing journal. On the left side, write uncomfortable situations, people's reactions, or hurtful statements you've encountered. On the right side, write how you can respond in the future to each. Underneath these columns, note how you can give yourself permission to ignore information that does not serve you.

How will you handle unsupportive comments or actions in the future?

Surviving the Milestones

"We think about you always, we talk about you still, you have never been forgotten, and you never will."

—Author Unknown

Milestone dates are an intense, emotion-filled experiences that will trigger acute grief. During the first year without your loved one, certain times can elicit the same intense pain as when the death occurred. Milestones can include any date that is significant, such as a birthday, anniversary of death, Mother's Day, Father's Day, Thanksgiving, or other holidays.

Here are some ways to honor your loved one and prepare for these special days with self-care.

Plan Ahead. Think about how you would like to spend the day. Would you like to spend it in quiet reflection or with others? Perhaps you would like to do something your loved one enjoyed? It is important to spend the day how you need to, not how others expect you to.

Allow Yourself Some Time Alone. The first important milestone may feel wrong and strange without the person you miss. You may have a hard time accepting that the person you care about is not with you like he or she was in the past. Allow yourself time alone to grieve and to not take part in any hustle and bustle that may accompany the day, if that is what you desire.

One winter after Mom died, I visited the cemetery on a cold, snowy, and dreary day. I don't remember the significance of the date or how long it had been since Mom died, but I remember the intense pain of disbelief that my mother was dead and that I was at a cemetery weeping for a death I did not expect or believe should have happened.

To help with situations like this, be gentle with yourself and set realistic expectations on how you may feel on important dates. Your most important task is to care for your emotional well-being and follow your needs.

Share Your Plans. Others may not understand the significance of certain dates without your loved one. Give them guidance on how they can help and welcome their support. Perhaps this year you would like to celebrate certain dates in a different way. Don't be afraid to break traditions so you can commemorate the milestones in a way that works for you. Keep your plans flexible. It's okay to leave your options open based on how you are feeling.

Involve Others. Would you like others to be involved in your plans for the day? Perhaps you need someone to go to the cemetery with you? Perhaps you want to get together with

select people to share memories? Perhaps you want a quiet
visit with a few trusted friends? Lean on your support network,
remembering that others want to help.

Holidays, special occasions, and milestone dates are the perfect
time to honor the life of the person you love.

- Would you like to place a memorial verse in
  the newspaper?
- Donate to a special charity?
- Plant a tree?
- Send flowers to yourself or other family members?
- Have a small ceremony at your house or the cemetery?
- Share special memories together over a meal?
- Look at photos or videos?

**How would you like to care for yourself while
honoring a milestone date?**

Making Progress

"Grief is about `relearning' the world."

—Thomas Attig

In addition to experiencing acute and subtle grief, healing can be experienced as a dual process. Researchers Stroebe and Schut found that mourners oscillate between being loss-oriented and restoration-oriented as they heal.[xiv]

Loss-oriented means to focus and process the pain of grief. You're experiencing the intrusion of sorrow. Loss-oriented activities include yearning, remembering, and reminiscing. Examples include looking at old photos, telling stories, and imagining how a loved one might talk to you.

Restoration-oriented means to attend to life changes, adapt to new roles, and form new relationships. You're being distracted from pain. Restoration-oriented activities include handling daily life activities and fulfilling the responsibilities of the person who died. Examples include cooking, taking care of children, maintaining the household, or managing finances.

Because grief is fluid, you may go from crying and being sad (loss-oriented) to learning how to pay the bills and mow the lawn (restoration-oriented). Sometimes you will face your loss head-on, and at other times you'll focus on the practical tasks of daily living.

You're realizing that you'll continue to live. You're learning how to plan for the future. You're learning how to problem solve. You're learning how to cope with small and large adjustments such as the following:

- How do I run the lawn mower?
- How do I pay the bills?
- How do I do laundry?
- How do I change oil in the car?
- Where will I find a job?
- Where will I live?

As you are coping with the changes in your daily life, notice what tasks are hard for you to do or what you don't like to do. As you identify these tasks, think about how to make them easier or eliminate them altogether. Be imaginative in how you problem solve. To get the hang of it, here are some creative ideas for addressing common problems.

I don't like getting out of bed in the morning and have a hard time starting the day. (Can I give myself something to look forward to? Plan a visit with a child or grandchild? Plan a morning commitment with a friend or colleague?)

I don't like Sundays because they are too long now. (Can I break up the day with an activity? Go to an upbeat movie? Go to lunch? Go to a park?)

I don't like going to church without my loved one. (Would going to a different service make a difference? Can I go with a friend? Can I sit in a different area of the church? Should I not go for now?)

My spouse always did the cooking. (Can a family member teach me? Can I purchase premade meals? Can a neighbor help?)

I never did grocery shopping in the past, and I don't like to go now. (Can I plan shorter trips to the store? Go to a different store? Order items online? Go with a friend?)

If you are having trouble with ideas to address your immediate issues, enlist a supportive person to help you as suggested earlier in this chapter.

In the initial months after the sudden death of the person you love, you'll be much more loss-oriented, but as time passes, you may spend more time in restoration-oriented activities. As you continue to adjust to your life without the physical presence of the deceased, you'll be discovering how to live in a different world. You may have a sense of helplessness or wonder how you'll get along without your loved one while you are simultaneously doing things you wouldn't have imagined you could do.

Actor Gwyneth Paltrow describes this dual process clearly. She once said, "I never knew I could suffer so much. And then, at the same time, you think; now I'm ready to open myself up to life in another way, to make it worth something and make it about the right things and not waste time."[xv]

Acknowledge each and every step you take forward, as you oscillate between loss- and restoration-oriented activities. Expand your focus on what is going right. For example:

Did you have a day without any tears?

Were you able to enjoy something today, like shopping or woodworking?

Were you able to relax with a companion?

Try this daily self-care practice: Noticing Your Progress. Observe your progress each day and record it in your grief healing journal. Here's a list to help you gauge your changes.

- I laughed today.
- I woke up, and the first thing I thought about wasn't my loss.
- I can look at photos without crying.
- I can sleep through the night.
- I am starting to eat better.
- I enjoy the present moment.
- I can go out in public and not be afraid of seeing someone or something that upsets me.
- I can tell my story without breaking down.
- I can help others.
- I can concentrate for longer periods of time.
- I am not as afraid.
- I do not cry as much.
- I can be in my home alone.
- I have periods of time where I forget about my grief.
- I can spend time with others and not be as sad.
- I sometimes feel happy.

As a survivor of sudden loss, you may not think you are making any progress toward healing. Compare how you feel at three, six, and twelve months from the date of loss to notice any differences.

What progress have you made?

Easing into Work Challenges

"Only the gentle are ever really strong."

—James Dean

Now that you've identified support for coping with daily life, let's examine how to get help when returning to work after sudden loss.

In our fast-paced society, you're often given the message you should be "back to normal" quickly. Of course, this is not realistic. Perhaps you aren't ready to return to work because you're apprehensive about talking to colleagues or fear crying in front of others. Perhaps you are wondering how to balance your additional responsibilities with your job or what effect your absence from home will have on family members.

I had a tough time returning to my job after Mom died. My supervisor hadn't talked to me about my absence, how I was feeling, or if I could handle my workload. Instead, it was business as usual, and I was assigned one of the most difficult assignments in our organization. I wondered how my supervisor could be so inconsiderate and uncaring toward my situation and feelings. Further challenging the emotional burden was the unnecessary stress of serving as a referee for two colleagues who were not getting along.

I could've had a more manageable experience if I had the tools or knowledge to adjust to my job and build a work support network. Instead, I ended up taking a two-month absence from my job after returning because I wasn't ready to deal with strenuous work responsibilities while new to grieving.

Honor your capabilities and energy level when you return to work. Talk to your supervisor honestly about your challenges and how colleagues may aid you. If coworkers impose critical judgments or unpractical beliefs on you, don't internalize or listen to them. Remember, you are the expert on how to best care for yourself.

To cope with new, unanticipated challenges about how you are feeling, you'll have to approach familiar work tasks differently to meet your needs. Consider these flexible work options to gently ease yourself back into your job:

- Shorten your workday if possible.
- Work from home for part of the week.
- Mix in shorter weeks by preplanning days off.
- Take a mini-vacation with a few consecutive days away.
- Work part-time for an extended period.
- Use sick time instead of your regular vacation days.
- Introduce a new work option to your supervisor.
- Take an extended absence from your job if possible.

If a flexible job arrangement is not possible, consider these strategies:

- Take frequent breaks.
- Take a longer lunch, using time to get outside for fresh air or a walk.
- Pace yourself. Work at a speed slower than you normally would.

Throughout the day, ask yourself, "What would make my job easier?" Listen carefully to what your inner self is telling you, and take action. For example, perhaps you need to close your eyes for a few moments, go outside for a short five-minute walk, take a break, or eat a snack. Imagine how you can accomplish your work and still meet your personal needs.

Try this daily self-care practice: Building Your Routine. Start a daily routine, which can add stability to your changed environment. Incorporate activities you enjoy or look forward to into your routine. A new activity can be started with one small thing you enjoy, such as a daily walk, morning coffee, or a hot shower with new shampoo. After work, perhaps journaling, viewing photos, meditating for a few minutes, or playing with your pet may appeal to you. For a weekend routine, Saturdays may be used to schedule a lunch date with a supportive person, and Sundays may be used to watch a movie. Spending regular, dedicated time in your healing sanctuary is an ideal way to build a routine.

Continue to add activities that are supportive to your routine. Pick and choose what suits you best. You will be taking small, loving steps toward healing. Reinforce your new routine by noticing if you feel more relaxed, balanced, or less overwhelmed.

What creative work options appeal to you?

Navigating the Grief Terrain

"Experience is a master teacher, even when it's not our own."

—Gina Greenlee

Now that you are more familiar with self-care and support networks, let's determine if other avenues of assistance may appeal to you.

A guide, coach, or teacher is an invaluable asset anytime you go through something new or want to learn a new skill. Going it alone, as you may be incorrectly encouraged to do, will simply slow or delay your healing. Leaning on those who have experienced the rough terrain of grief prior to you will give you hope and possibility that better days will come. A guide, coach, or teacher will know where the stumbling blocks are and can provide valuable assistance.

Consider seeking a role model who is further along in his or her healing or a grief support group, spiritual counselor, or resource material. To find a guide:

- Ask a friend or family member for a recommendation.
- Consider those you have admired for their resilience.
- Identify those who have suffered a sudden loss in your circle of friends, colleagues, or neighbors.

I didn't have a mentor to model how to integrate loss into my life when Mom died. Due to my young age and inexperience in seeking support, I didn't initially understand assistance was an option. Over time, I gradually began to seek help despite my fear and apprehension. Several years after Mom died, I met a health care provider who offered a refreshing view on loss and healing. She encouraged me to continue the bond of love and keep Mom's spirit alive through my actions. Her guidance was a turning point in my healing, and now I understand how invaluable support is to surviving a sudden loss.

Attend a meeting at a support organization.
Professionals and volunteers are ready to assist and listen to you. It's essential to have the guidance of those who know grief. Others who have experienced the sudden deaths of those they love are living proof that you will survive. Access to support programs can increase your confidence as well as decrease depression and hopelessness. Help can come from many sources, including programs through your funeral home, hospices, bereavement organizations, grief counselors, therapists, online forums, or social media.

Research options for help. Do an internet search to identify what type of healing support is available in your community. Local hospices, funeral homes, and community organizations will list upcoming grief support meetings on their websites. Alternately, reach out to a friend, colleague, or neighbor to ask for a potential recommendation. To explore the option of individual support from me, visit my website. I'd be honored to talk to you, hear about your beloved person, and offer personalized support.

About three weeks after Mom died, I attended a support group at a local church that was suggested by a friend. I was nervous about going but needed to talk to someone so desperately. I trusted my friend's advice, yet berated myself for needing to be in such a group at all. Sitting in the church parking lot, parked near the entrance, I hesitated, and waited, and waited, unable to go in. I was so afraid that if I was asked about my situation, I wouldn't be able to hold it together in front of the others. My fear was paralyzing. But it was getting me nowhere. So I opened the door. *How bad can it be?* I thought.

Once inside the meeting room, a sweet-faced nun welcomed me. Her comforting demeanor, and the way she showed me where to sit, immediately put me at ease. I was in a room with about twelve other people who recently had people they love die. Oddly, I didn't feel uncomfortable, but felt I'd found a new group of friends who understood. I still remember the group members and their guidance twenty years later. In fact, this was one of the most helpful forms of assistance I received.

Read books about grief healing. Check out books from libraries, borrow periodicals from support groups, or browse the selection at a local bookstore or online. By learning more about sudden loss, you can gain insights on how to cope with emotions and what to expect. Hard-earned wisdom from those who have survived the death of someone they love may help in ways your immediate support system cannot.

One of the most valuable gifts I received after my mother died was a grief healing book that I still own to this day. At the time, I read small excerpts most evenings before trying to sleep. The words brought comfort and understanding to my heart. This special book was my companion, bringing light, hope, and encouragement at a very dark time. I hope this book does the same for you.

What other types of assistance may help you to navigate grief?

Practice Four

Reconnect: Develop Ongoing Spiritual Connection

Healing Grief with Spiritual Presence

"However painful it is to bid farewell to one who has died, once you have done so, you begin a new relationship with them, one you can always cherish. Once you release them from earthly time, you can embrace them in eternity. When you release them from the physical dimension, you can hold them close in a dimension no less real the spiritual one. For even though they no longer walk beside you, they will be even closer."

—James E. Miller

Love never dies.

Love is eternal.

Love transcends even death.

Because the bond of love is never broken, you can use the power of love to reconnect with the deceased. Reconnection invites you to move forward and find fulfillment by developing an ongoing spiritual relationship with your loved one. While physical death may mark the end of one phase of a relationship, you can continue to build an even stronger bond of love by reconnecting to the person who died. It's possible to discover a renewed relationship through spiritual connection. Love remains and is the most powerful energy of the world.

Let's begin. When a person dies, his or her physical body stops functioning, but energy continues and passes into another dimension. Your relationship with your beloved is transformed from physical to spiritual. His or her soul continues to live beyond the physical world. There is no restriction of space or time on soul energy. Since the deceased is not limited to a material form, he or she is free of pain, worries, and fear. "There is no death. There is only a cycling and recycling of energies—a changing of form," explains Louise Hay, deceased author of *Heart Thoughts: A Treasury of Inner Wisdom*.[xvi]

Your beloved person's energy continues to exist in another realm to watch, guide, and protect you—but, most importantly, to continue to love you. The departed's soul is closer to you than ever before. Your loved one's spirit knows your deepest feelings, thoughts, wishes, and desires and is aware of what is happening in your life. Souls in the spiritual realm know how to comfort, reassure, and support when called to do so. It's your choice to reconnect and cultivate this connection at any time— including right now. You have the natural ability to tap into this loving, energetic presence.

"Spirits are connected to us through love. They hear us. They feel our emotions. When we mourn for them, they feel our pain. When we pray for them, they hear our prayers. When we honor and remember them, they feel that, as well. And, when we need them, they may come to our rescue in their own way, from the other side," explains Mark Anthony, author of *Never Letting Go: Heal Grief with Help from the Other Side*.[xvii]

Your beloved's spirit is not gone.

The deceased's love did not vanish.

Your relationship continues.

However, you may struggle to publicly hold onto the relationship with a beloved person because of cultural messages to cut ties alongside pressure to move on and get back to normal. Just because someone is dead does not mean your bond or feelings die. You don't "get over" the love. Remember, the person you love will always continue to be an important, enduring part of your life and will continue to be even after you die.

Your heart is meant to love, and there is no limit on the number of people you love, including those in the spiritual realm. By reconnecting, you are not preventing healing, but instead, you are living with loss while keeping your loved one close in your mind, spirit, and heart. The healthy resolution of grief involves maintaining a continuing bond with the departed, instead of severing the tie, disengaging from the deceased, or letting go of the relationship.

You will be together, always.

Whether you believe it or not.

Whether you feel it or not.

Whether others doubt it or not.

You may be skeptical. You may not have faith. You may wonder how. You may fear others' reactions. I am often asked by clients how I know "for sure" beloved people continue in another place. I have experienced many signs and incredible communication from those I love. And I can undoubtedly tell you that believing in reconnection was the most critical component of my grief healing. I've experienced perspectives on the depths of love that I never dreamed possible.

When connection and continuing love is cultivated, you can heal grief and become whole again. I found it was much easier to accept physical death when I learned I was receiving divine guidance from those who died before me. Their undying love and continued presence provided great comfort, peace, and healing. I learned death was not absolute. I now understood my departed loved ones were not gone forever, but with me forever. Even death cannot separate love.

But like you, I am an ordinary, everyday person without any special superpowers. When I was new to sudden loss, I knew nothing about the afterlife. I was a layperson, not a medium or psychic. I was hopeful my loved one's existence could continue in some way but had no evidence or belief this was possible. I often wondered where my deceased loved ones were.

As time went on, I began to read books on the afterlife which gave one astonishing story of connection after another. Over time and with the help of mentors, I began to expand my understanding of the spiritual realm and use of intuition. I began to welcome and develop a reconnection with my departed loved ones. I learned death does not end a relationship.

I chose to give myself permission to accept the symbols and messages I received as true.

I chose to trust there is a higher power far beyond what one can understand in the material world.

I chose to believe the departed's spirit continues to exist in a vast, boundless form.

I now choose to share my numerous experiences as well as many others' remarkable recollections to provide inspiring evidence that relationships do not end with death. As author Martha Whitemore Hickman so eloquently explains, "Wherever our loved one has gone, our love has followed. And surely that love is reciprocated. Sometimes it seems almost palpably in the room with us. What is at work here, we do not know. We do know that love binds us to the dead and they to us—in stretchable, but not breakable bonds."[xviii]

When it is time to leave this world, you'll be reunited in another more perfect and divine place where you'll exist in eternal light and peace. You'll return back to love itself, a home you've forgotten. Until then, you can reconnect in a new, albeit different, way. It is not necessary to say goodbye, but hello to the spirit of your loved person.

Your beloved is ready to hear from you. Your love has not been lost but is waiting to be found by you.

How can you welcome the spirit of the one you love now?

Using Spiritual Connection

"I imagine you smiling in heaven—pain-free, problem-free and perfectly content to wait until our Reunion Day. My heart fills with gratitude that our loving God will make that day a reality."

—Diane Pursley

It may seem impossible, but you have the gift to tap into your loved one's presence using your intuition. For many years, I did not know the ability was available, but, once I did, a whole new world of healing and understanding opened. I wish this for you too.

Choose to open your heart and mind to this possibility of reconnection.

You determine the time for your reunion when you are ready. Reconnection can be at this very moment.

You hold the power.

You can reaffirm your continuing bond with those who died through the power of love. As author Jim Miller eloquently explains, "They will be within you. And you will not forget them because you cannot forget them. They will be as near to you as your own breathing and as much a part of you as your own dreaming. They will exist in you as love."[xix] Eternal love will serve as a guiding light as you nurture spiritual connection.

I teach my clients and students that everyone can learn to reconnect with those they love who have died. You can build your connection muscle by trying out various exercises presented in this chapter whenever you like. Some exercises you can use as a daily practice, or others you can try just once. Some exercises can be used during your time in your healing sanctuary, and others can be used as you go about your daily life. Whatever you choose, the goal is always the same—to open your heart and mind to the possibility of reconnection to heal grief. Let's start.

Try this practice: Seeing Sparkling Eyes and Shining Smiles. To begin your reconnection, close your eyes, and breathe deeply for a few moments. Go to the center of your being and open your heart toward giving and receiving love. Begin to feel deeply your beloved person's love for you in this moment. Imagine this love flowing from the spiritual realm as a bright, peaceful light surrounding your heart.

Recall the best memory you had with your dear one, whether enjoying a fun time, sharing in an accomplishment, celebrating a milestone, planning a wedding, or enjoying the birth of your child. Focus on the scene as if you were there right now. Relive and feel the emotions as if they are happening in this moment. Employ all your senses. See your loved one's eyes sparkle with love, imagine his or her wide, shining smile, hear his or her joyous laughter, and feel the soft touch of his or her hand.

Remember the feelings of pure joy and bliss you had together. Recall the love you felt and received from this moment. Breathe deeply and let this wonderful feeling wash over you.

As you relive this love, you'll store this emotion in your cellular memory, which contains your body's ability to retain memories, sensations, and experiences. This beautiful, loving feeling is accessible to you at any time and any place you allow it.

When I do this exercise, I imagine an old, faded photo of my parents in which they are smiling widely and their eyes are twinkling, shining brightly. As I look at their faces in my mind's eye, I begin to feel a tingling sensation, sometimes on my left temple, top of my head, or between my eyes. This soft peace is their unique energy coming to me. I feel their unending love and blessings. When you're open to it, you can feel similar sensations too. The gentle peace and healing you'll experience may inspire you to use this practice regularly.

By reliving fond memories, you'll be able to feel pure love and joy, which raises your energic vibration to a higher level and brings the spiritual realm closer. You are tapping into your loved one's presence. You'll begin to know and understand he or she is always near, constantly close when you call, and always there to support you.

The loving, wonderful feeling you have for another being becomes ingrained in his or her soul, just as it is embedded in your heart.

You are a part of your beloved's heaven, and she or he is a part of you.

You are rooted in each other for eternity.

**If you believed in the spiritual presence of your loved
one, how would this change you?**

Noticing the Signs

"It's only with the heart that one can see rightly; what is
essential is invisible to the eye."

—Antoine de Saint-Exupéry, *The Little Prince*

If you are like me, you want to know if the person you miss is
at peace, happy, and okay. You may have asked, "Is my loved
one really in heaven?" or "Is her spirit still with me?" You may
struggle with these questions and look for proof and validation
as I originally did.

"It is the physical loss, the loss of a touch, the loss of speaking
to our loved one and hearing them answer, and knowing that
we will never be able to hold that person again in this life that is
so hard for most people to accept," explains Kathleen Mathews,
coauthor of *Everlasting Love, Finding Comfort Through
Communicating with Your Beloved in Spirit*.[xx] She says, "The
love bond grows even stronger without the limitations of the
physical body. Your loved ones can connect with you easier
than ever before once the physical body releases the soul.
All the senses—like touch, smell, sight—can still be achieved
physically through our being aware of our loved one's presence
near us every day."

Each person has a different way of connecting with the spiritual
realm, whether through a combination of feelings, images, or

sounds. You've likely experienced numerous subtle signs from spirit that you've been missing. For example, you've probably experienced the chills or have had a strong gut reaction, which is a form of clairsentience (meaning a clear feeling of sensing).

Perhaps you have heard words, sounds, or music in your head. Or you've heard a subtle sound or entire phrase. This is a form of clairaudience (meaning clear hearing). Alternately, maybe you "knew" something for no apparent reason. This is a form of claircognizance (meaning clear knowing). Finally, perhaps you've seen a vision flash through your mind, much like a daydream. This is a form of clairvoyance (meaning clear seeing).

Try this practice: Focusing on the Background and Noticing the Signs. Close your eyes and listen with concentration. You'll hear sounds and sensations you simply haven't noticed before. Do you hear appliances buzzing, a furnace or air conditioner humming, your house creaking, clocks ticking, a pet breathing, or birds chirping? The point of this exercise is to show you there is more going on than you normally perceive.

Continue to sit in silence with as little background noise as possible.

Reflect upon these questions:

- Have you felt your loved one being close to you?
- Have you seen spiritual signs at unexpected times or places?
- Have you felt the person you miss provide comfort and reassurance?

As you think about these questions, gently cultivate gratitude for the person you love. Open yourself, including your eyes, ears, nose, sense of touch, and inner knowing, to have the answers revealed. Continue to remain quiet and still. Observe the sensations you feel.

- Do you see anything with your eyes?
- Do you hear anything with your ears?
- Do you smell anything?
- Do you sense or know anything?

Don't disregard the answers, feelings, or hunches you receive. Listen to what your internal guidance or navigation system is saying. You'll begin to notice how you receive guidance, and it may occur in more than one way, whether your senses or inner knowing. Continue to practice this exercise. The more you notice and focus, the more you'll perceive and receive.

Perhaps the spirit of a person you love is with you at this very moment, next to you, above you, below you, or only half a step behind you. Perhaps he or she is waiting, desiring, and preparing to help you. Perhaps he or she is doing everything possible to let you know he or she is next to you. This loving soul is around you, near your side, entering your thoughts, and answering your prayers to serve as your helping guide.

The deceased's spirit has entered into a whole new world that cannot be comprehended by us. His or her spirit is evolving and growing in ways we cannot imagine. Perhaps you can let the mystery unfold naturally and surrender to the unknown, while setting aside everything you've been told or believed in the past.

After writing this chapter over a year ago and revisiting it now, I am amazed by how my spiritual senses continue to expand. I receive communication every day through sensations on my body, usually accompanied by an inner knowing or familiarity.

I usually get these feelings when something fun or wonderful is happening. I also get distinctive feelings when I am trying to make a decision or an idea enters my mind that requires action. It's a spiritual confirmation of a "yes" to guide me.

How have you sensed the presence of your beloved person?

Imagining Heaven

"Maybe my heaven will be living as a memory in the hearts of those I loved."

–J. Iron Word

I worked with a bereaved mother who found great relief in imagining her son in his new home, which she believed was heaven. This woman was not at the accident site when her child died, and, for a long time after his death, she kept replaying her son's death over and over in her mind by imagining the scene of his accident. These intrusive thoughts caused her an unending loop of suffering.

Instead, when she began to imagine her son in another place— cradled in the palms of God—and no longer at the accident, she was able to shift her perspective and curb her disturbing thoughts. By changing her mind's narrative, she came to a new, more tolerable vision of her son and where he is now. She learned how to direct her thoughts to foster healing rather than perpetuate harm.

Try this practice: Peeking into the Windows of Heaven. To continue building your sensory messages, practice this exercise now or use it during your daily time in your healing sanctuary.

Relax and open all your senses. Notice how your eyes, ears, nose, and body feel. Pretend you have a glimpse of heaven. Even if you don't believe in a higher power or heaven, imagine a place where your loved one's essence resides—a home that's safe and secure where he or she is happy.

Now peek into the window of this wondrous place where earthly hurts are left behind. See the beauty, feel the warmth, and hear the celestial music. You spot your beloved, who looks so young, healthy, and strong. The person you love is free of aging, illness, and physical ailments. Imagine he or she is calling your name, waving at you, smiling, and sending the message that all is well. You know your cherished one is tranquil, serene, and free. Your precious one is at peace.

Draw on your powers of intuition and inner knowing to answer these questions:

- What if you knew without doubt your beloved is okay and not alone?
- What if you believed the person you love is no longer in pain or sick?
- What if you understood your dear one's love for you is stronger than it ever was before?
- What if your loved one wanted only fulfillment, happiness, and joy for you?
- If you believed the answers to be true, how would you feel? Would you feel loved, cared for, and blessed? Would you feel relief, comfort, or acceptance? Would you forgive yourself or the person who died?

Notice how your mood lifts, even if for only a minute, when you think about your responses to these questions. Record your feelings in your grief healing journal.

What do you see when you imagine heaven?

Try this practice: Receiving a Message from Spirit. Close your eyes and become quiet, still, and introspective. Continue to think about the treasured person you miss in the loving, serene place you just imagined.

Say aloud, quietly, "I can no longer see you with my eyes, touch you with my hands, but I feel you in my heart forever. If you could give me a message, what would it be?"

Perhaps your deceased loved one would say:

- I will always watch over you, protect you, and guide you.
- I will love you forever.
- It's not your fault.
- I'm proud of you.
- Go on and live.
- I'll be by your side.

I know Mom would give me this message: "Remember, I love you. I have always loved you and will continue to love you. Even when you can't see me, I will love you."

I believe Dad would say, "I love you. I'm sorry I had to leave you. It was not my choice, but it was my time. I am pleased that you and Mom could go on and make a life worth living—a life you can be proud of."

I imagine the children I lost through miscarriage would say, "We love you, Mommy. Even though you didn't get to meet us in the physical world, we love you. You learned lessons from us that only we could provide by leaving your body. You are sharing the messages of hope, love, and ongoing spiritual connection with the world now because of your deep losses. But remember, you did not lose us; we are with you every day."

I trust your message would be a similar one of never-ending love and eternal life—a confirmation that love lives on, spiritual connection is real, and your beloved person is near. Write the message from your loved one in your grief healing journal or on the margins of this page. Turn to it often to bring comfort and peace.

What's your message?

Asking for Without a Doubt Signs

"A recipe for miracles: one dose of intention, a pinch of focus, and a whole lot of faith."

—Unknown

To prove spiritual connection is real, psychic medium and author Karen Noe encourages asking deceased loved ones for "without a doubt signs" to connect with spirit energy. When you are patient and wait, proof will arrive. I've personally learned signs and communication will come in surprising and delightful ways when I ask for them.

After asking for a "without a doubt sign" from Mom, I received a response quickly. I was driving to the library to work on this book, and I saw a license plate that said, "MOM DN." I interpreted this to mean my mother, Donna Nancy, is helping me write this chapter. On the way home, I saw another license plate that said, "MOM ON." Over the next two days, I continued to see license plates with different versions of the word Mom, including "MOMIK" and "41MOM." Previously, I had never noticed license plates that say "MOM." I laughed as I thought, "Mom is giving material for my book."

Many months later after these initial signs, I continue to receive more communication from both Mom and Dad, often through messages on license plates and billboards. Messages seem to be more easily received when I am driving since I am in a more relaxed meditative state. Sometimes messages just pop out to give me reassurance that spirit is close or to provide reminders of things I need to do.

For example, the other day I noticed a license plate that said "258" at about nine fifteen in the morning. I typically call my elderly stepfather at nine o'clock to check on him, and I had forgotten. His phone number starts with "258," so this was spirit's prompt to call him. Later that same day, when I was picking up my son from camp, I spotted a license plate that said "WRKSHP." This was a reminder to sign-up for a workshop I wanted to attend.

Later, I received another message on a license plate that said "DRU." This was a prompt to call my bookkeeper, Dru, to follow-up on an outstanding computer issue. Like many people, I have lots of responsibilities between work and family, and sometimes need friendly reminders to keep me on task. Who knew I would receive assistance from the spiritual realm!

For more specific guidance, I will sometimes ask a question and wait for the answer to appear in whatever form the sign manifests. I ask questions about everyday things as well as more important matters. Amazingly, the responses often appear within minutes. It's like playing a game!

One day I asked, "Do I really need to make this video?" I was applying to coach employees about personal growth at a large organization, and the potential client wanted a video about my credentials. I was busy and tired. I didn't want to go through the effort but wanted the gig. Sure enough, when I was driving, I saw a sign on the side of a truck that said, "There are no shortcuts."

"Ugh!" I thought, "Now, I have to make this video." I did, and I received the coaching engagement two weeks after submitting the video.

What "without a doubt" sign will you ask for?

Becoming Familiar with Types of Signs

"Goodbyes are only for those who love with their eyes; for those who love with heart and soul there is no separation."

–Rumi

Loved ones communicate through a myriad of signs. As you've already learned in the book, some messages come from one's senses, such as thoughts, feelings, scents, and sounds. Physical signs can come from objects, electronic items, nature, and animals.

Have you ever had the following occur?

- Billboard messages appear to pop out at you
- License plates convey a message
- Random book passages or magazine articles contain just the information you need

- Street signs surprisingly show your loved one's name
- Conversations from strangers apply to you
- Butterflies or birds appear when you are thinking of your beloved
- Rainbows appear when you need inspiration
- Lights or electrical items flicker on and off with no explanation
- Meaningful objects appear before you, such as pennies or feathers
- A distinct scent reminds you of the person you miss

When you receive such a message, give yourself permission to believe it. If you think it is a sign, it is. It doesn't matter what others believe. If a sign gives you comfort and peace, consider it a gift from your beloved person. Focus on what makes you feel good.

Mark, whose partner of forty years died almost one and a half years ago, was receiving many signs from his soul mate. He was finding lots of pennies, but all of a sudden, to his dismay, the signs and pennies stopped. Mark was sitting outside looking at the chair where his partner always used to sit and asked, "Why don't you leave pennies anymore?" That night, Mark felt two taps on the back of his neck and the next morning there was a penny under his partner's chair. Later, he was having a difficult day and put his head on his kitchen table and cried, saying "I miss you so much." When Mark got up and went by his mate's picture on the wall, there was a penny on the floor directly under the photo. The penny was from the year they met.

Try this practice: Asking for a Sign. It's simple. When driving or going about your day, ask a clear question and wait for the response to appear in the next twenty-four hours. If you are trying to make a decision, ask, "Is the choice to _____

optimal for me?" Fill in the blank with your desire, whether
it's to buy a car, move to a different home, switch jobs, or start
something new. The answer will come in a way you'd likely
not expect.

You may receive guidance in many ways, such as: overhearing
a conversation, noticing a verse in a song, hearing a phrase
on the television, seeing a headline in an ad, reading a fitting
passage in a book, spotting a message on a street sign, finding a
meaningful object, remembering a vivid dream, or observing a
significant animal.

When you continue to ask for signs, your spiritual connection
will strengthen as you become more familiar with receiving and
interpreting messages.

What types of signs have you received already?

Thoughts

How many times have you wondered, "Is my loved one really talking to me?" Spirit communicates through frequency or energy. All matter is made of atoms. Atoms have a specific vibration which has a frequency. This frequency is used for communication. It's like tuning your radio to a certain channel to pick up the signal.

You may communicate with a beloved person through energetic thoughts. It's like when you know what a parent, partner, or friend is going to say before they say it. Examples of signs through thoughts may include:

- Having an answer pop into your head when you need it
- Receiving guidance when daydreaming
- Knowing just where to find a missing item
- Obtaining ideas out of the blue
- Receiving a gut instinct or feeling about a person or situation

Try this practice: Spirit through Communication. It's not hard. Consider it an experiment. Start a conversation with your beloved person. Simply say, "How are you today?" You may feel a dialogue begin. You can talk aloud or in your head. You are asking for more than a message. You are beginning an actual back and forth conversation.

Talk about whatever is burdening you or troubling your heart. Say whatever you need or want to say. See the person responding as you talk to him or her.

You may think you are using your imagination and the connection is not real. Instead, trust the flow of what you say and receive. You may feel a sense of peace, safety, or well-being wash over you. Note what comes to you in your grief healing journal or in the margins of this page.

At any time you can use this exercise—it becomes a useful tool to converse with those you miss, whether you're spending time in your healing sanctuary or having a bad day. You'll likely feel better by expressing your emotions and thoughts.

I often talk to my deceased parents silently. I will start with "Hi, Mom. Hi, Dad. How are you?" and then see what thoughts suddenly develop. I ask them questions and tell them what is happening in my life. I seek guidance, feel love, and ask for validation about being on the right path. I let the discussion progress naturally without questioning, judging, or censoring. Occasionally, I capture the conversation with pen and paper.

As I was writing this book section, I synchronistically found a piece of loose drawing paper hidden away in a binder of notes. On this paper, I had previously recorded the first conscious dialogue I had with my father more than forty years after this death. I had forgotten about this note.

I recalled that when I was yearning to know more about Dad, I had a stream of thoughts come to me suddenly. I grabbed a pen and quickly wrote:

My dearest Chelsea,

How I miss you. I am so sorry I had to leave you so soon because that was not my intent. I love you and only wanted to be with you. Your mom and I wanted you and only you from the very start. I had other things I needed to do. I know you wish it were different, and it will be different because I do love you from here. I miss you and your little arms around me—the love of a child only for a father. My love is always yours, and you'll always have it.

Watching you from above,

Love Dad.

I was shocked and dumbfounded when this information came to me. I received a divinely orchestrated message. I was beginning to learn how to communicate with my father and to understand he was only a thought away. I had wanted this validation and communication for so many years, and when I was finally open to it, the connection came. This can occur for you when you open your heart and mind to the infinite possibilities.

With repetition, experience, and openness, you'll notice how spiritual connection unfolds and develops for you. Remember, this connection grows gradually and can take many months and years to build, just like a relationship in the physical world. You can also work with a local intuitive counselor, psychic, or medium to validate the messages you receive when you're ready. This interaction will develop your confidence to know you're receiving real, credible information. Ask for a referral from a trusted friend or check the service provider's references to ensure he or she is the right fit for you.

Try this practice: Spirit through Imagery. It's relaxing and calming. Close your eyes, take a deep breath and imagine a vibrant, budding pink rose. See, smell, and imagine the flower. As the petals of the bud open, picture your beloved's spirit in the center. What does he or she look like? What is he or she wearing? What emotions do you feel? Love, peace, or joy? Go toward the person, look him or her deep in the eyes, and hug each other tightly. You might want to talk, cry, laugh, or just feel his or her presence. Allow this loving interaction to occur naturally without skepticism. Give yourself the gift of experiencing the spirit of your loved one.

When you're finished with your time together, let your beloved know you'll visit again soon. Watch the rose's smooth pink petals close. Open your eyes and allow the healing energy to wash over you. As you repeatedly use guided imagery, you'll become familiar with your loved one's comforting presence, which you'll learn to summon. Record your interaction in your grief healing journal, noting any important details.

As you continue to have more conversations, record and date them in your journal. Revisit your journal often to observe any emerging patterns of information.

What spiritual communication have you received through your thoughts?

Sense of Touch

Have you ever felt a deceased loved one close to you, but disregarded it as wishful thinking? Perhaps you've felt a slight touch on your hand, a brush of your hair, or the perception of someone sitting near you. This sensation is the presence of spirit.

You may feel or hear a family member enter a room or walk up or down steps without seeing them, but know who it is. Similarly, when a person has shifted from physical to spiritual form, you can still sense who it is.

With signs originating through the sense of touch, you may experience a change in energy, perceive actual movement, or feel slight pressure. When I am in a relaxed state, I will simply feel peace, safety, or well-being suddenly wash over me. Although the sensations seem to appear out of nowhere, I attribute them to spirit comforting me.

From when I was a little girl until I was about a freshman in high school, I would feel a light, reassuring tingling on my right forearm occasionally. As an adult, a medium confirmed this experience was a sign from my father. Dad was letting me know he was near and watching over me. In one of my father's last photos, he was kneeling next to me with his arm around my back and his hand on my right forearm. His hand was in the same spot where I felt the calming sensation as a child.

Try this practice: Spirit through Touch. It's simple. Ask spirit for a sign you'll recognize. When you feel an unusual sensation, slight pressure or chill, stop, take in the feeling, and ask your intuitive self what the message is telling you. Perhaps your beloved is letting you know he or she is near, providing confirmation of an answer, or just giving you a reassuring hug. Trust your inner guidance. Note any signs you receive in your grief healing journal.

What signs have you received through sense of touch?

Songs

How many times have you heard the perfect song with the perfect message at the perfect time? Perhaps you've turned on a radio and a special song is playing to remind you of your loved one. Perhaps you've heard background music at a store, restaurant, or work, and the lyrics provided just the right message. Or, you've heard a song in your head, for no reason, that reminds you of the deceased. Don't chalk it up to coincidence; it's a message from spirit.

About ten years ago during the start of the holiday season, I received my first recognizable message through song from Mom. One evening, while sitting in Jacob's nursery, I realized how lucky I was to have this new baby to enjoy Christmas with. After having a miscarriage, I wasn't sure if I would ever have a family of my own, and now I did.

Since Mom died right before Christmas, I hadn't been celebrating this time of the year with joy. I'd even made a habit of not looking forward to it during the past ten years. But this year was different. I had a new baby. And since Christmas is about the celebration of birth and new life, perhaps it was possible this season could be different. I was open to a sign.

Jacob's room was warm and comforting, the walls a faux finish with a lovely combination of blue, yellow, and light pink that I had painstakingly selected to create the perfect room for my child. The blue-sky ceiling played off the white wooden rocker, crib, dresser, and bookshelf filled with fun kids' books. This was a room I would have loved to show to Mom.

I got an intuitive hint to listen to Sarah McLachlan, my favorite singer since Mom had died ten years earlier. Sarah's latest CD, *Winter Song*, had just come out, and I popped it into Jacob's music player and listened as we snuggled on the floor. "Have Yourself a Merry Little Christmas" came on, and, upon hearing the chorus, I knew.

This was it. The sign. Mom's spirit was telling me to go on. That it was okay to enjoy Christmas again, especially with my new child. Christmas had arrived early that year—the day that I banished self-doubt and learned that it is indeed possible to continue to connect and communicate with loved ones. Forever. And that was the best gift of all that Christmas season.

Now, I feel her presence often. I feel my mom's spirit when I hear songs by Roy Orbison, one of her favorite singers. I also know she is near when I hear the songs, "Tainted Love" by Soft Cell and "Always Something There to Remind Me" by Naked Eyes. One evening after working all day, I wasn't looking forward to going out to dinner. But then, right when I sat down with my stepfather at the restaurant, I heard "Always Something There to Remind Me," and I appreciated the surprise that Mom would be joining us. Most importantly, I knew Mom was supporting me as I continued to help my stepfather with his challenging health issues.

Try this practice: Spirit through Song. It's simple. Ask for a sign through song. Turn off the music you have playing. Later, when you have forgotten about this exercise, you'll have the urge to turn the music back on. When you do, listen to the lyrics, and you'll have a personal message. Use this exercise anytime. If you'd like, jot down the messages you receive in your grief healing journal to help you take note of any patterns of messages.

I recently used this exercise, and, sure enough, when I later turned on the radio, I heard "Always Something There to Remind Me." The message was a reminder that Mom will always be a part of me. I love when I hear the songs that represent Mom as they are always a pleasant, joyous surprise.

What songs have messages for you?

Animals

Have you wondered if animals are signs from your loved one? Seeing physical signs from an animal or winged insect is a common way to receive spiritual communication. Since loved ones exist in a form of energy, they can direct the force of animals and objects. Cardinals, hawks, butterflies, and dragonflies are commonly reported as messengers.

Tammy, a client whose partner died a few years earlier, was in her vegetable garden thinking about how she missed her beloved Doreen. Because they loved gardening together, she felt especially lonely and anxious. To Tammy's delight, a dragonfly suddenly appeared, and she just knew it was a sign from Doreen. Tammy raced into her house to get her camera and, amazingly, the dragonfly was still there when she returned. A few minutes after she took the photo, the dragonfly flew across her face and its wings fluttered gently on her nose. "It felt like a kiss, just like Doreen used to give me," said Tammy, beaming. This tender feeling calmed Tammy and filled an empty space in her heart that day.

A bereaved granddaughter who was a client of mine reported a cardinal pecking at her windowsill every morning shortly after her grandmother died. She knew it was her grandmother coming to visit her. Although she didn't understand how she could know such a thing, she chose to trust her intuition that her interpretation was true. Similarly, a family of three adult children who had recently lost their father reported seeing large black crows at their parents' house and their own homes each day. They believed the crow was the perfect symbol for their father's unique personality and characteristics.

Spirit can also give you specific messages through animals. One morning when I was at my desk contemplating a significant career move, a large bird hit my window and startled me. I knew it was a sign to make the change. This occurrence scared me, especially because I am afraid of birds. I asked spirit not to repeat such a disconcerting sign. Today, as I am writing, I saw five small gray and white chickadees outside the same window. They were calm, gentle, and friendly, and represented how I view and receive spirit connection.

Try this practice: Spirit through Animals. It's easy. Ask spirit to give you a sign through an animal. Sit back and wait. When you receive this message, stop, take in the moment, and contemplate what the special communication means. Note your sign in your grief healing journal to detect any patterns of connection.

What animal signs have you received?

Scents

Have you ever smelled something suddenly for no reason and without a logical source? These can be signs from spirit. You may smell the scent of perfume or tobacco; food you associate with a loved one, such as a favorite meal or dessert he or she made; or a scent that instantly connects you to a favorite memory.

For example, I smelled the fragrance of my mother's perfume suddenly outside of my office when I was working and there was no one nearby. I loved the scent and appreciated the comforting presence of Mom. Another time, I was with a health care practitioner for a Reiki session and smelled tobacco.

This long-forgotten scent from over forty years ago suddenly triggered reconnection with my father. When I would hug my dad as a small child, he would bend down to my eye level, and I smelled this same scent, his tobacco in his front shirt pocket.

I was enjoying an afternoon outing at a favorite lake. While my son and I were walking in a heavily wooded area, I smelled lilies—the flowers I used for my wedding. Of course, there were no flowers to be seen and, on the return trip a little while later, the fragrance was gone. I attributed the scent to Mom being present with me on a long-awaited, needed day away. She knew I loved this scent. It occurred at the same time I was writing this section of the book, so I could share my experience with you.

Try this practice: Spirit through Scent. It's easy. Ask spirit to give you a sign through a scent. Simply ask and wait. When you come across a unique scent that reminds you of your beloved, stop and savor the fragrance. Ask yourself what the sign signifies. Note your experience in your grief healing journal.

What signs have you received through scent?

Photos

Seeing evidence of your loved one's image in the background of a photo is another way to receive a sign. Many people have reported seeing the likeness of loved ones or images of angels and orbs, which are transparent balls of energy in photos. The photos may have to be held at just the right angle for the images to appear to others.

When my colleague and I were offering a grief support workshop, *Joyful Grieving*, we needed promotional photos.

We decided to write messages on balloons to our deceased loved ones and then release them. The final photos of the balloon release showed many small orbs surrounding us. We were amazed! The spiritual realm was shining through in our pictures. We believed we were getting support and praise for our work.

In a photograph of Jacob and me from a few years ago, Mom is making an appearance. We take an annual picture each May by a blooming crabapple tree to capture its magnificence and compare Jacob's height from year to year. In the photo, a distinct likeness of Mom appeared behind the tree in the background. This remarkable image is framed in my living room. I delight in seeing this tangible reminder of Mom's loving spirit each day.

After author Dr. Wayne Dyer died, his family spread his ashes in the secluded waters near his home in Maui. The likeness of his face appeared in the water's waves. The family captured this silhouette in a photo and his publisher shared this amazing image with the public. Even after he died, Dr. Dyer could show others that the soul lives on.

Try this practice: Spirit through Photos. It's simple. Ask spirit to give you a sign through a photo. Examine new and past photos from special occasions. Since spirit loves to share in meaningful times with you, notice what evidence you discover. Look for background images, shadows, or smudges that appear out of place in the photos. You may be pleasantly surprised to see loved ones joining in the festivities. Note your discoveries in your grief healing journal to track evidence of spiritual reconnection.

What images have you seen in photos?

Objects

Have you ever found a unique object and wondered if it was a sign? Finding feathers, coins, stones, charms, or small physical objects is another way for spirit to communicate. Typically, these are objects you can't miss or that have a special meaning. Framed pictures that move, objects that drop in front of you, or items that you keep misplacing can be signs.

A bereaved mother discovered a small angel charm in a busy area where small kids were catching buses after school. It was no small feat to find this metal charm with the number of curious children who could have found this shiny object first. More astonishing, however, was that this woman's aunt, who lives hours away, sent her a gift basket with the exact same charm. The bereaved mother believed the angel charms were a sign from her young daughter who had recently died unexpectedly. She later cast the charm into a gold pendant to wear each day to keep her child's spirit close.

I've also received unique objects from spirit. One day, I was wondering where Mom lived as a child. Since her parents were not alive and she was an only child, I thought I'd have a hard time finding the information. Shortly thereafter, much to my delight, I had the urge to look at old pictures. In a family photo album, I saw a worn, jagged newspaper clipping of my mother, who was fifteen, painting a portrait at a local art show. In the article caption, Mom's name, Donna Wiese, and address were given. Suddenly and synchronistical, I had the information I wanted!

Recently, I was wondering the date my father died and wanted to know the answer. Since I was a little girl when Dad died and Mom didn't talk about him, I didn't know the dates of his birthday or death. The next day, I stumbled upon an old, metal-hinged box of mementos tucked away in an extra bedroom closet. In this long-forgotten box, I discovered Mom's worn datebook which listed people's names and birthdays. Unfortunately, it didn't have my father's birth date. After rummaging through the box more, I discovered Dad's death certificate. I also found a tattered business document showing his birthday. I was thrilled to find this information. This was a box I had not opened for years, but I found just what I wanted through a little divine guidance.

I've also received useful gifts from spirit. I was having a difficult time decorating a certain corner in my kitchen, and my stepfather had sent me a flowering tree for Mother's Day. He typically sent flowers, but this year, he sent this unusual gift. This tree was just the right height, the flowers were just the right color, and the pot was just the right size pot to solve my decorating dilemma. I chalked it up to decorating advice and a gift orchestrated by Mom. Now, this special tree sits in my office as I write these words to you.

Try this practice: Spirit through Objects. It's not difficult. Ask spirit to give you a recognizable, unique object as a sign. When you find an interesting item or notice something unusual, ask yourself what the message denotes. Note your experience in your grief healing journal.

What objects have you encountered as a sign from spirit?

Electrical Items

Have you seen lights, televisions, or other electrical appliances flickering and wondered if they were messages from your beloved?

Televisions, radios, clocks, lights, and phones can be affected by spiritual energy. Electrical items can turn on and off or move positions for no logical reason. Clocks can stop at the same time each day and continue to flash the identical time. Televisions and radios can change channels or stations without explanation. Doorbells can ring for no reason. People have even reported receiving telephone calls from numbers that have significant meaning with static or no one there.

Recently, my friend's mom, Nancy, who lost her husband, Dick, sent me a thank you letter for sending her the book, *When Heaven Touches Earth*, which is a compilation of people's stories, including mine, who have received spirit communication. After receiving the book, she was inspired to share one of her experiences of spiritual signs with me.

Nancy described coming into her living room the day before her deceased husband's birthday and relaxing in a recliner after a long day of yard work. Her table lamp, which Dick built, had the light bulb flash on and off. The bulb would light up, dim, and come on again. She thought, "Okay, dear." She checked the switch, which was off. The cord was plugged in properly. Nancy knew immediately it was a sign from her husband, giving her a thumbs up for her hard work while taking care of the yard. She said, "Yes, Dick, I know it is you."

A few years ago, I was interviewed as one of the authors from *When Heaven Touches Earth* to share my experiences of communicating with deceased loved ones. While I was waiting for the phone interview to begin, I asked my loved ones and spirit guides to join me. The ceiling light in my office began flickering and burned out. This had never happened before, and I knew it occurred due to the energy in the room. I previously had not received signs like this, so I was delighted to receive this spiritual confirmation.

Another time, I was hosting a recorded phone interview with an intuitive healer for an online grief healing seminar I was sponsoring. The phone line kept going out, and we had to reschedule the call for another time. The healer believed the line was not working due to the energy interference from her spirit guides and the souls of her deceased mother and grandmother, who she talks with often.

Try this practice: Spirit through Electricity. It's easy. Ask spirit to give you a recognizable or repeatable electrical sign within the next day or two. When you have an uncommon electrical occurrence, ask yourself what the sign means. Note your observation in your grief healing journal.

What unusual things have you encountered with electrical items?

Numbers

Do you ever wonder why you see the same repeating numbers? Numbers can symbolize spirit is near, represent a significant date, or denote a meaning in numerology, which studies the relationship between a person's life and numbers.

You can keep waking up at the identical time in the middle of the night to see the same numbers on your digital clock. You can see repeating numbers on just about anything from license plates, receipts, and addresses to phone numbers, clocks, and taxi numbers. You can also see repeating number sequences such as 111, 222, or 333.

A grieving mother who lost her sixteen-year-old son to bone cancer often sees her son's favorite number, forty-four, which adorned his football jersey. A client reported seeing two license plates with her birthdate and her deceased husband's birthdate. She knew these were signs from her husband who had an affinity for numbers when he was alive. I see license plates with the number 772, which represents the month and year of my father's death, as well as the number 118, which represents the month and day of my mother's birthday.

Try this practice: Spirit through Numbers. It's easy. Simply ask spirit to give you a sign using numbers. You'll likely know what the number signifies. Alternately, you can determine the numerological meaning of repeating numbers with a simple internet search. Note your observations in your grief healing journal to identify any patterns.

What repeating sequence of numbers have you noticed?

Dreams

Have you felt your loved one come to you in a dream? Have you questioned if he or she was really visiting you? There have been many reports of people having visitations from deceased loved ones in their dreams. Typically, a dream is called a "visitation" if a loved one's spirit comes to you while sleeping.

Visitations differ from ordinary dreams because they seem real. You may gain peace or receive a special or important message. In a visitation, your loved one may look younger and healthier. The deceased may appear at their favorite age or when the person liked his or her physical appearance best.

Many years ago, Mom visited me in a 1970s-styled outfit during a dream. Her appearance made me laugh as there is no way I would have chosen her outfit or hairstyle. During another dream, I had a visitation from a family friend, Catherine, who had just died. Catherine had decided to discontinue dialysis and knew she would die shortly after stopping the treatment. Her life revolved around the treatment of her illness, so she was ready to leave the physical world even though her family was not. In my dream, I sensed how Catherine felt when she was dying, and I validated that her decision was understood by her loved ones, although she was missed terribly by her family.

Betty, who was twenty-three when her mother died on Mother's Day, shared her dream experience. "It was more than a dream," explained Betty. "I went to see my mother in the afterlife. I walked through the front door of heaven and hugged her. She said I had to quit grieving because it was making me sick, so I must stop. I asked if my room was here and she said yes, but the bed was not made. It was a little joke because I never made my bed. I remember smiling and laughing at this. However, it really meant I wasn't ready for heaven yet," says Betty.

"I was so happy to see my mother. I felt all this love, which seemed like it was from many. I did not want to leave. But a voice came and said I had to go, so I was forced back. I woke up in my bed in distress because both of my legs were cramping. It seemed like I had been where I was too long because I didn't want to come back. I remembered everything. I knew I was told to stop grieving, so I did. It was easy for me after that because I had seen and talked to my mother," recalls Betty.

"After my dream, I always felt she was close, and I just didn't feel sadness again. I was blessed with a healing gift from God, so I believe grief does end. My mother was in a different place, and it was beautiful and full of love and peace. As the years go by, I realize I was very fortunate to have this experience and to feel the beautiful love," says Betty.

Try this practice: Spirit through Dreams. Before you go to sleep, ask a beloved person to visit you in your dreams. When you've had such a visitation, immediately record any vivid details upon awakening. Note any special messages, observe how your loved one looked, and reflect upon any symbolic meanings. By recording your observations quickly in your grief healing journal, you can prevent forgetting important details and have the information to review later.

What comforting dreams have you received?

Not Sensing Signs

"To believe in the things you can see and touch is no belief at
all; but to believe in the unseen is a triumph, a blessing."

—Abraham Lincoln

You may be thinking, "That's nice that other people receive
signs, but I haven't. Is there something wrong with me? I've
asked, begged, and prayed, but still receive nothing. Don't I
deserve a sign, too?"

Yes, you deserve a message—a love note from your beloved
person who died. You are already worthy, and do not need to
make yourself anything more. Your loved one wants to be in
your presence just as much as you want him or her there. No
matter where you are, you are not alone. Spirit is always right
by your side to see and hear you. The person you love who
died is working to send you the message that he or she is okay,
you're deeply loved, and you're not alone.

When you are in deep pain and distress, it's harder to receive
comforting messages. After your unexpected loss, your head
is foggy, your energy is depleted, and your heart is heavy.
You may be lost in your own world and unable to clearly
comprehend what is going on around you.

When you are in sorrow and most need a sign from heaven,
your low energy vibration does not match the high energy
frequency of the spiritual realm. As you begin to heal
emotionally, physically, and spiritually, you'll have more
moments of joy and relaxation. As you experience higher
vibrations from elevated emotions, you'll be able to connect
more easily with those you miss.

In the first months of mourning for my mother, I cried and slept a lot, suffered headaches, and didn't eat much. I survived on orange juice and chocolate chip cookie dough. I wasn't thinking clearly. I didn't sense any signs and was not in any condition to receive them. However, as I reflect upon my experience now, I did receive subtle hints and nudges from the universe, but they were not detectible to me at the time.

Try this practice: Spirit through Asking. It's as simple as it sounds. Ask spirit for an understandable, meaningful connection. Declare aloud or say silently to yourself, "I am ready and willing to receive messages, signs, and communication from you. I am open and eager to receive your love, guidance, and protection."

Believing and trusting in your ability to connect to the spiritual realm will facilitate signs. If you focus on being unable to receive contact, you'll likely not receive communication. If you ask for messages to come in a specific form, you may be disappointed because they often come in unexpected, astounding ways. But, if you intend for spirit to communicate with you, you'll have your intention met in unique, remarkable ways.

About fourteen years after Mom died and my son Jake was a toddler, I asked her to confirm undoubtedly that she was still with me. Within two weeks, Mom's cousin, who I didn't know well and had only met a few times, called me out of the blue and offered to give me a set of antique crystal glasses that were my grandmother's. Mom had always loved to buy me special presents, and was I flabbergasted when I received this meaningful gift divinely sent by her. I was shocked by how quickly my request for confirmation was answered. I am still amazed by this magical occurrence and now know the power of asking for reconnection.

Keep an open mind and eye to start observing what is around. You may be surprised. At times when you feel relaxed or calm, you're more likely to notice an unexpected, subtle connection. I have experienced almost all the types of signs in this chapter, and it gives me a sense of being supported and guided.

Now I have daily spiritual communication, but this came over time with conscious intention, practice, and understanding. By becoming familiar with how your loved ones communicate with you, you'll be able to reconnect and develop an ongoing spiritual relationship.

Try this practice: Spirit through Receiving. To nurture your ability to sense gifts from the universe and loved ones, begin a receiving section in your grief healing journal. To start this process, write, "I have received the following signs today: _____" Now, for the next seven days, notice what messages you receive. At the end of each day, take a few minutes to recall the signs you noticed. Record these gifts in your journal and note the date.

You'll see evidence of spiritual support mount as you begin to fill this section of your journal. The purpose of this exercise is to facilitate your belief that you are not alone, your loved one is with you, and the universe loves and supports you.

How can you trust in your ability to receive signs?

Using Meditation

"Meditation is the tongue of the soul and the language of
our spirit."

–Jeremy Taylor

Use meditation to facilitate communication from the spirit
world. You may not have realized you meditate every day
through routine, repetitive activities such as driving, showering,
walking, or listening to music. When you are driving, and
wonder, "How did I get here so fast?" you were meditating.

Your subconscious mind takes over when your mind is engaged
in other activities. When you want to connect with spirit, you
can relax your mind by slowing your thoughts. You may think
it is too difficult to get your thoughts to subside, but with
practice it will get easier. The more you meditate, the more
you can enhance your connection to your loved one in the
spiritual realm.

Try this practice: Spirit through Meditation. First, find
a quiet time and place when you will not be interrupted by your
family, phones, or work. Your healing sanctuary is an ideal
place to do this. Wear comfortable clothing. Sit in a relaxing
chair. Keep your back straight, feet on the floor, palms up, and
eyes closed.

Begin breathing deeply in and out to a count of four. Breathe in
a fresh breath of life. Release any tension in your body, letting
it fall away with your breath. Feel your body getting lighter and
more relaxed. Imagine any thoughts in your mind floating away
like clouds.

Imagine a column of divine light coming down from above you and moving gradually through your body, starting at the top of your head. Feel the light move through your eyes, ears, neck, shoulders, chest, solar plexus, legs, and feet. This column of energy continues deep into the center of the earth and then slowly rises back up to your heart. You are now connected with divine energy from above and below you.

As you continue to breathe, feel this warm, loving energy in your heart radiating out and surrounding you. This spiritual energy loves you exactly for who you are, knowing you are perfect in every way. There is nothing you must do to gain this love—it is present for you now and always. Imagine with each exhale you are releasing any barriers to this loving energy, and you're able to feel this love and light even more.

Now, imagine you are going to a beautiful place. It can be anywhere, whether in nature or inside. It can be somewhere you've been before or a place you create now in your own mind. Where are you?

Feel what it's like to be in this magnificent place. Look around in all directions and notice the amazing beauty. Notice the temperature of the air. Is the air warm or cool? Is it moving or still? Notice what you smell. Is there the scent of trees, flowers, or fresh air? Reach out and touch something in this place and notice the sensation.

Now, invite in your spiritual connection—a spiritual presence that loves you unconditionally. Imagine this divine energetic presence coming toward you from the distance or appearing suddenly in front of you. The presence can come in many forms, whether it's your deceased loved one, an angel, an archangel, a divine teacher, an ascended master, Jesus, Mother Mary, or God. The connection can come as an older person, a child, or even an animal or butterfly. It does not matter—accept whatever image comes to you. If no figure is emerging, begin to imagine different loving presences that are comfortable for you. Begin to observe them and pick one that feels right to you. Just relax and explore this connection.

What are you seeing or feeling?

Breathe in the love that is radiating from this spiritual presence. Just take in the love through your breath. This spiritual connection sees the beauty and magnificence of who you really are—and treasures you. There is nothing you need to do or say to earn this love. This spiritual presence is there for you, just like the air you breathe.

Now, see if your spiritual connection has a message for you—something that is important for you to know right now. Just breathe and let the message flow to you naturally.

What is the message?

When you are ready, you can say goodbye to your spiritual connection in whatever way feels right to you—knowing that you will be reconnecting again soon—whenever you need or want to. Take a moment and record your experience in your grief healing journal.

You can reconnect with this presence at any time during the day or night. The more you practice this meditation, the stronger your spiritual connection will become. You can rely upon this presence as a source of unconditional love, support, and guidance.

How will you use meditation to support your healing?

Using Prayer

"A single grateful thought toward heaven is the most perfect prayer."

—Gotthold Ephraim Lessing

A daily self-care practice that can be useful to you is prayer. No matter what your belief system, prayer can provide encouragement and hope as you heal. You can use prayer whenever you like, even in your healing sanctuary. Prayer can help you release unprocessed emotions and cumulative grief. Research shows that prayer can help with restoration by reducing stress chemicals and improving unhealthy behaviors.

Prayer can range from praying for ourselves, the person who died, or others who were affected by your loved one's death. Offer a prayer for the person you miss and give thanks for the many blessings you still have in your life. This will not lessen your loss but may help you consider the other things that make your life worthwhile.

There is no right or wrong way to pray. Do what feels right for you. It can be a thought, a feeling, or the voice of care.

A prayer can be as easy as saying, "Please renew my spirit as I sleep and take away my fears," or "Release any fear-based thoughts I have," or "Send me the answers to my questions."

Or you can simply send love, light, and blessings to other individuals through prayer. You may not know this, but it's likely that others have silently prayed for you too.

When a friend lost her one-year-old child, I prayed for the family with written prayer. I simply wrote the person's name

I was praying for and what strength I wished them. You can do the same for yourself—pray for what you need—whether it is hope, faith, love, or renewal. Write it in a designated prayer section in your grief healing journal.

Let your prayer take the form that most comforts you.

Try this practice: Spirit through Prayer. Close your eyes, lower your head, and say a prayer aloud or silently. Start with "I bless you with pure love and light" and let your words flow naturally. Pray for the person you miss. Pray for your family. Pray for a renewed spirit. Pray for the capacity to reinvest in life. Pray for the ability feel the spirit of your beloved. Pray for answers about life and death. Find comfort as you rest in the arms of a higher power.

How will you use prayer to support your healing?

Practice Five

Reassess: Discover Meaning and
Purpose from Loss

Noticing Your Growth

"When we come close to those things that break us down, we touch those things that also break us open."

—Wayne Muller

You may already understand you are irrevocably changed by sorrow. Even though you may yearn and wish for things to stay the same, the death of someone you love becomes a catalyst for life change and reassessment. With grief comes personal growth and transformation, whether it's wanted or not.

You've been knocked off course and, when you gain your footing again, you'll begin to wonder how you fit in and who you are in this new place. You'll be forming new perspectives on life and love. You'll be reassessing how to rebuild your life going forward without the physical presence of your beloved. You'll be learning how to live with loss.

Like others who have walked the path of healing, you have the resiliency and capacity to reenter life. But you must choose to live again. Only you can make this decision.

Although you may feel ill-prepared and ill-equipped for this challenge, you will be uncovering strengths, traits, and perspectives you never knew you had to rebuild life while simultaneously mourning and loving the person you miss. This chapter walks you through the practice of reassessing life to discover new meaning and purpose.

With grief as a teacher, you may be gaining:

- increased compassion and empathy
- more sensitivity toward others

- an increased consciousness of time
- a lack of interest in trivial matters
- an appreciation for each day
- a new passion toward life

While you're alive, you'll continue to grow, progress, and evolve, but when you're in pain, you may see the change as unwelcome. Even so, you'll find new interests and adapt to different directions in your life as you continue to be shaped from your loss.

This growth through grief evidences you're alive. Like the changing seasons, life changes and transforms, too. Real pain leads to deep change.

How have you changed—positively—since your loved one died?

Viewing Today as a Gift

"This is not a dress rehearsal. This is it."

—Tom Cunningham

The real lesson of sudden loss is that you thought there would be more time to talk, make amends, and really love those you care about. You learned the hard truth that life is precious and death escapes no one. Sudden loss teaches you the value of what matters.

You have likely discovered:

- You have only this one precious life to live.
- You have only the present moment.

- You have no do-overs or second chances.

Life does not offer permanence and change is constant, although our expectations are much different. You may agonize about the plans you should've had with your loved one and fear a future that needs to be rebuilt. While you're worrying about what is yet to come and finding sorrow in the past, the present moment is moving quietly away. Death is a powerful reminder to live fully and choose better if you can let it.

As I begrudgingly let go of the longing to go back to the way things were before Mom's sudden death, I began to gradually reenter my changed world. This rebuilding was challenging. I remember being in the foggy cloud of grief, but sometimes I would have instances of brightness—appreciation of the little things. One summer day, I recall marveling at the sun, the sky, and the flowers. I noticed kids playing with their mothers, smiling and laughing. I saw my husband's twinkling eyes and heard his mischievous laugh. These were glimmers of light during a dark time that I hadn't noticed before.

Although you may not be able to appreciate "the now" while mourning, treat moments of each day as gifts when you can.

Perhaps you can cultivate gratitude for being alive.

Perhaps you can focus on how you want to live.

Perhaps you can appreciate the small gifts you're taking for granted.

These suggestions are not meant to deny your hurt or pressure you, but instead prompt you to think about how you might savor small moments of life and be present to them. You are giving yourself the opportunity to think about what you do have instead of exclusively thinking about what you don't. Although it may not seem conceivable yet, when you do the inner work of healing, you'll reengage in life and discover profound meaning. In time, new possibilities will arise while keeping close the love of the person you miss.

Try this healing practice: Living On. Close your eyes, take three deep cleansing breaths, and imagine that you want to "live on" and recreate your life to honor the person you love who died. Answer the questions with the first thoughts that come into your mind.

- What do you desire right now?
- What would you really love to do?
- What have you always wanted to do but have been afraid to try?
- Where would you like to reside or travel?
- What unfinished projects or dreams would you like to complete?
- In what ways can you add meaning to your life?
- How can you authentically live your life?

If you have a hard time answering these questions, you're not alone. Give yourself time and space to contemplate your future. You may be used to bypassing your wants to meet others' expectations, dismissing your desires as "unrealistic," or substituting the "rational" goals of others as your own. But now, after loss, you can choose what you want if you allow it.

Use your dedicated time in your healing sanctuary to think about these questions. When in moments of silence, your habitual thoughts and worries are subdued and the voices of others are quieted. Answers from deep within yourself can arise as you connect deeply with yourself.

Are you spending your time how you would like to? If not, what is holding you back?

Living Life Authentically

"While we live, let us live."

—D. H. Lawrence

When you experience the sudden death of someone you care about, you'll begin to see the world in a new and different light. You'll continue to experience unexpected, life-altering changes, and these adjustments can be frightening and confusing. Change can feel unsettling, unnerving, and unpredictable. At the same time, death is a powerful wake-up call, telling you that it's time to start living life differently—better.

I remember feeling like I was cracked wide open when Mom died unexpectedly. My relatively safe world had been crushed instantly, and the pain was soul-shattering. Emotion after emotion erupted in my broken being. My true, real feelings rushed through me like a tidal way. Nothing was held back, and I wondered if the wild emotions would ever stop. Mom had died, and I was in shock and disbelief.

Suddenly, nothing else mattered.

You may feel broken, too. Your heart may ache in places that you didn't know existed. You may feel you are in a deep, dark pit of despair. When the intense pain of loss breaks your heart wide open, your true inner self and emotions have a chance to break free.

You can take advantage of these previously hidden, forgotten feelings to reassess your life now.

In loss, you find your authentic self.

The authentic self is who you are before limiting beliefs and societal expectations are learned—it is the self you naturally are. It's who you were born to be before you learned to hide your opinions, feelings, and beliefs to stay safe in the world.

It's the freedom to follow your soul's calling before the doubts and opinions of others seep into your being and change how you begin to act. The authentic self is your internal compass to direct you to a purposeful life of your dreams. It's the opposite of what you "should," "must," or "ought to" do.

The authentic self is demonstrated through the compassion you have for the heartache of another and the genuine sadness for your loss. It's seeing life through the eyes of a child, the giggles of a toddler, and the awe of a baby discovering something new. It's the tears of joy when your children are born and tears of sorrow when they leave your home. It's the organic love, joy, and peace you feel in your heart. It's not the learned responses of shame, doubt, and guilt.

After the loss of Mom, the woman who was my rock, I was reintroduced to my authentic self. My true self had gradually, unnoticeably faded away as I was influenced by cultural and family expectations of what I "should" do. Now, I felt very brave and courageous, like a child who was fearless before she was taught about danger.

My existence as I knew it had ended. I knew that nothing more awful could happen, so I gained a sense of empowerment and a lack of fear. I reasoned, "The worst has happened, so anything else will be nothing. I am already in a living hell." Through the holes of my heart, my genuine feelings were starting to rise, giving me a new, stronger sense of myself. Courage was born in my pain.

I was learning to rebuild my life authentically on my terms, not others'. I was jolted out of my comfortable, conditioned world due to the shock and devastation of physically losing the person I loved and continue to love. I woke up.

In tragedy, I received my life back. But this awakening was achieved the hard way. I would trade in all the lessons of loss to have my loved ones back. The choice I made was to make the most of my remaining life.

My suffering would have worth.

I began to follow the promptings of my heart and pursued what was right for me. The real, whole me, which was always inside, was emerging from the brokenness. I wanted to live a no-regrets existence. This was a turning point due to the death of someone I loved and a loss I wish would have never occurred.

You, too, can use your loss to identify what is most important to you right now. Ask yourself, "What do I really want?" Remember these raw, uncensored thoughts and feelings because they will fade as pain lessens. Even if you can't act on what you want right now, capture this vital information because it's essential to your future life.

How can you live your life better, honoring your true self?

Cultivating Desires

from Your Authentic Self

"There lives in each of us a hero awaiting the call to action."

—H. Jackson Brown, Jr.

The midst of sorrow is where you are the closest you've been to your authentic self since you were a child. The needs and wants from your true self provide a trail to uncover your life direction after loss. Perhaps you may already know where you want to be, but don't have the energy or resources to get there yet. Perhaps you know you want something different, but don't know what it is yet.

Be mindful of your genuine desires that are surfacing and contemplate how you can incorporate these into your life. Pay attention to these feelings, and act on them now or when you are ready. Trust that what you are realizing about yourself today will help you determine your future life choices.

You may wonder how you've become so separated from your true self or traveled so far off course. Western society does not teach people how to build relationships with their inner selves or honor their hearts' desires. For example, your parents may have modeled withdrawal from their real, true selves. Your family may have had generations of detachment from their feelings and wants, leading you to learn the same unconstructive behaviors.

As you grew from childhood, you may have become disconnected from your inner spirit to form a false, conditioned self. This is the façade you present to others to shield yourself from their opinions, criticisms, and judgments. This protection is used to navigate the world to fit in with societal and family expectations in order to avoid shame and embarrassment. This false, conditioned self is not your real, true self. It's how you've adapted to the circumstances around you to survive.

The consequences of being disengaged with your authentic self can include:

- Fear and anxiety
- Lack of trust in the future
- Depression and hopelessness
- No sense of purpose or meaning in life
- Feeling alone
- Addictions

You may have experienced some of these symptoms, which can become more prevalent when mourning. The false, conditioned self mirrors many of the untrue cultural messages about how to handle grief (quickly, quietly, and alone) that cause more suffering. The feelings of guilt and shame, which are produced from your false, conditioned self, make mourning and grieving more arduous. However, when you are operating from your authentic self, you can allow your natural feelings of sorrow, loss, and heartbreak to be expressed and released. Like an onion, you are peeling back the protective layers to reach your core.

Because you're in closer alignment with your natural authentic self when working through sorrow, you can uncover honest, sometimes hidden, answers to what you need. Your true desires will surface, not the conditioned, programmed, or family-expected answers. For the first time in a long time, you may be free to notice what you really want to do with your precious time on earth.

Try this healing practice: Imagining Your Future. To identify the desires of your authentic self, pretend you're ninety years old, sitting on your front porch. It's a sunny day and you feel a warm breeze. You hear birds chirping, a dog barking in the distance, and the laughter of children in a neighboring yard.

You are reviewing your life, seeing it roll by year after year. You're imagining and feeling many wonderful events. You're thinking about what you care about and your most important relationships. You feel safe, content, and peaceful. You feel satisfaction from the great life you lived.

As the fascinating images float by, you're doing things that matter, devoting time to what you enjoy the most, and spending time on meaningful work. What do you see? What are you doing? Who are you with? Record these images in your grief healing journal. Label it "My Future Self" and review this vision often to guide your actions.

What one step can you take now to align yourself with the life you imagined?

Try this healing practice: Dumping the Junk. Close your eyes and take a few calming breaths. Imagine, see, and feel in detail what your heart truly wants. Revisit the image of your future self. Notice how it would feel to have your life just how you'd want it. Now, think about what is blocking you from your desired life. Is it a person? Is it a past experience? Is it the lack of energy or time? Is it a false belief, doubt, or fear? Is it a trapped emotion?

See whatever is preventing you from moving forward. Imagine a large yellow dump truck arrives in front of your home to take away everything that is holding you back or standing in your way from living your life authentically. Throw all your junk into the back of this huge truck. Once you have emptied your heart and mind of these limitations, watch the dump truck drive away. Notice how you feel more peaceful now that these burdens have disappeared.

What do you genuinely desire for your future?

Answering the Important Questions

"Nothing is worth more than this day."

–Johann Wolfgang von Goethe

When someone you love suddenly dies, you'll naturally start thinking about life and its meaning—where you are in life, what you desire from it, and what's missing. You may ponder the universal questions of why you are here and what is the purpose of life. These queries are common and should not be ignored, but instead examined to discover your unique answers. The meaning you find or assign to your existence will not be like any one else's.

Loss will call for a reevaluation of your priorities and how you use your precious time. What once drove your actions, such as acquiring material possessions or advancing your career, may have much less value after you suffer the unexpected loss of your beloved. You may regret that these past goals took your time away from the people you love. You may realize now that time is your most prized possession.

I didn't appreciate what was good in my life until sudden death struck my mother. I was young, only twenty-eight, and had the luxury of time and energy to change my life from this unwanted wake-up call. Pain was an invitation to free myself and reclaim my life. It was a second chance to move forward in another, more fulfilling way.

I immediately knew after Mom died that I was on the wrong path for my career. Although I was previously aware of the problem, I never slowed down to assess what was happening. I was too busy chasing promotions and accolades, even at a young age. Not necessarily because I wanted the rewards, but because I was doing what I was "supposed to do." I was unhappy, unsatisfied, and stressed. The job, travel, and related drama seemed meaningless and foolish after Mom's death. I regretted how it took losing her to bring me to this stark realization.

Shortly after Mom's death, I sat on my living room couch with the sun shining on my face, telling my concerned husband that I was going to quit my corporate job. I needed time to myself and couldn't deal with my toxic work environment which was magnified by my strong, unyielding grief. I could no longer power and push through. I had no choice but to slow down, rest, and take care of myself.

My husband was afraid and believed we couldn't afford to have me leave my full-time, seemingly successful position. In retrospect, we could have. We were young and didn't understand the many life choices and possibilities that were available to us. My husband was in fear, and his worry triggered my fright of another enormous life change. So I continued to work, despite my apprehension.

I knew it wasn't the right decision. I felt resentful of my spouse and my choice to go along with his wishes when my real self was screaming at me to act otherwise. I knew better. But I stayed in the mode of marching through time and going through the motions. My authentic self, however, kept reminding me of the decision to stay in a situation that did not support my needs. The pain was calling me to change.

I knew what was right for me, but I wasn't acting on it yet. There was an undercurrent of feelings reminding me, shouting at me, to do something different. I would hear, "Chelsea...this is not right. Change it." I was starting to retrieve pieces of my real, authentic self. The parts of my soul that I had lost were coming back to me bit by bit.

What seemed like eons (but was only three and a half years) after Mom died, I finally left my corporate career to fill my aspiration of being an entrepreneur. It was time to do the things I wanted to do. I took the leap. I took the chance. It was risky. I was scared, but it felt great! I was living on my terms. I was doing exactly what I wanted. I was being true to my heart.

I opened a gift and home décor store in a quaint small town in Wisconsin. My shop was born in a ten-room, two-story 1868 restored house. I had about 1,800 feet of selling floor with eight employees. For me, it was a dream come true. I was using my natural talents and abilities in a business that was right for me.

It took time for my feelings of desired change to manifest into my reality. I wasn't able to act immediately on what I wanted after Mom died because of the physical and emotional challenges of grief as well as financial fears. But I was able to make a shift and change my life positively after I was further along in grief healing. The authentic, real feelings that came spilling out when death struck stayed in my heart. This constant reminder to live life on my terms kept returning to my mind.

I loved running my gift store. It was my baby. After five years of owning my business, surprisingly, I became pregnant. Being an only child with deceased parents and no extended family, I was thrilled to know I would finally have a family of my own. But this dream was not to be.

About eleven weeks into my pregnancy, I had a miscarriage. I was devastated and crushed by this profound, abrupt loss. My heart was cracked open again, and the strong desire for my own family came to the forefront. I was thirty-seven and knew what I needed and wanted. My priorities had changed again. I decided to sell my successful store and focus on myself to heal from the death of my unborn child.

But now, unlike when Mom died, I was able to act on what I needed and did it without hesitation. Only two and a half months after leaving my store, I was pregnant again with another baby, my son Jacob, who is now the light of my life.

Try this healing practice: Identifying Your Heart's Desires. Answer these questions and record your responses in your grief healing journal:

- If you only had six months to live, what would you do?
- Who would you spend time with?
- Where would you go?
- What would you change?

You may want to spend more time with your kids, visit your childhood home, or reconnect with someone you haven't talked to in years. You may want to move, go back to school, or switch careers completely. You may want to embrace your natural talents to volunteer, take up a hobby, or start a new venture.

Perhaps you want to live truer to yourself, express your feelings freely, or enjoy life more. Perhaps you want to live each day as if it were your last—a day to be remembered. Perhaps you just want to wake up and live. The choice is yours each day.

How can you allow yourself to express yourself?

Finding Passion and Purpose

"You have a unique message to deliver, a unique song to sing, a unique act of love to bestow."

—John Powell

Your priorities become clear when someone you love suddenly dies. Grief changes your inner world. You may crave deeper, richer meaning in life. You'll grow and change in new ways and may want more significance, value, and purpose in your life. You may want to make a difference, make an impact, or shine your unique light.

But how do you do this? How do you find purpose after loss?

You need to uncover and engage in what you're passionate about. Think about:

- What makes you come alive?
- What did you enjoy in the past?
- What would make you excited to start the day?

Your passions give life meaning. Pursuing your natural interests and promptings will lead to more purpose and fulfillment in your life.

Try this healing practice: Discovering Your Passion and Purpose. Take out your grief healing journal and write your immediate response to these simple, but powerful questions to gain insight into your passions.

- What one thing would you stand up and fight for?
- What makes you mad?
- If you could give a two-minute message to the world, what would it be?

To illustrate, a client said she would stand up for her children and was angry when people weren't kind and respectful. She believes the world needs to educate adults and children on how to treat each other with dignity. This was her passion, and it was reflected in her life's work as a mother, a social worker, and an elementary school employee. A bereaved mother, who had recovered from cancer, now coaches others about healthy lifestyle choices. By serving others, she is reinforcing her desire to live a healthy, long life.

Maybe your calling is to educate others on a challenge you or your loved one had, such as cancer, heart disease, diabetes, or depression. Perhaps your goal is to inspire others to be healthy through meditation, raw foods, or natural remedies.

What is your passion?

Exploring Your Inner Self

"Don't ask what the world needs. Ask what makes you come
alive, and go do it.
Because what the world needs are people who have
come alive."

–Howard Thurman

As you heal, you'll continue to learn about yourself—your
desires, values, and priorities. Allow time for inner growth and
examination. As you become introspective, you'll find clarity
about your unique talents, passions, and purpose and what
you'd like to do in the future.

Set aside time every day for exploration of your inner self as
you move forward. This is an ideal activity to do during the
dedicated time in your healing sanctuary. As you identify
areas of interest, learn more and investigate possibilities. Note
insights in your grief healing journal.

**Try this healing practice: Identifying Your Unique
Talents**. To determine your natural strengths and gifts, ask
friends, family, and colleagues to share your top three strengths
or talents. If you're uncomfortable asking for feedback face-to-
face, ask through an email or text. Choose only those people
who you trust and think highly of you. Because your talents
seem so simple and natural to you, others will share attributes
you've taken for granted.

When I did this exercise years ago, I was described as caring,
compassionate, supportive, highly sensitive, intelligent,
and business savvy. I was surprised by some of the answers.
A few of these strengths seemed regular, ordinary, and

downright boring. But your inherent traits are unique, amazing gifts, especially to those who don't possess the same unique characteristics.

What are your unique talents? How can you offer your gifts to others?

Try this healing practice: Identifying Your Natural Inclinations. Your childhood activities are a key indicator of your unique abilities and gifts because you did what came naturally and was fun. Recall what you loved to do. Did you like playing sports, performing in plays, building things, creating art, or helping others? Look at old pictures for clues of how you spent your time. Ask a parent or grandparent what you enjoyed doing if you can't remember.

For example, since I was a young child, I have enjoyed art and creating items. I especially liked making gifts for people. When I was in elementary school, I made crochet potholders, macramé plant hangers, decorative stones, clay flowers, and just about any popular 1970s craft. I liked to admire the beauty of my creations and then give them away. For me, giving gifts was just as exciting as making them. In high school and college, my skills became more advanced, and I began selling wall hangings and decorative T-shirts.

By remembering the activities I liked as a child, I could discern what I would enjoy as an adult. My love of art and giving presents led me to owning a gift shop and my current online sympathy gift store. I offer meaningful memorial gifts to remember loved ones, and I get to create products, including my Hello from Heaven series of gift books. This aspect of my business fulfills my needs to create, give, and assign meaning to the loss of those I love.

What activities did you enjoy as a child that you could incorporate into your life now?

What are your unique gifts and natural inclinations?

Bringing Joy into Your Life Gradually

"Joy does not simply happen to us. We have to choose joy and keep choosing it every day."

—Henri Nouwen

The reason you are identifying your unique talents, gifts, and passions is to learn how to bring more joy into your life while healing. Your natural state is joy, and it cannot be lost. You can uncover joy deep within yourself when you embody and practice it. Joy is part of your true, divine self, which feels many emotions such as peace, love, acceptance, compassion, and gratitude, along with joy.

But when you're in grief, how can you feel any pleasure? Your capacity for joy has been naturally deepened by your overwhelming sorrow. Your ability to fully feel all emotions, even positive ones, has been expanded. Your perception and sensitivity have been heightened. After experiencing the lowest of lows, you'll be equipped to savor and truly appreciate the highest of highs.

Happiness can occur, even if it's shadowed by sorrow.

Joyfulness is possible, even if it's wrapped inside the hurt.

Joy and grief can exist simultaneously. It's not all or nothing.

It's okay to allow both tears and joy. Consciously fostering and bringing joy into your life is not meant to push away or cover up your painful feelings, but to empower you to know that you can have pleasurable moments despite your underlying grief. You are allowing yourself to be human and to experience the full range of emotions. By practicing joy, you are taking another step toward healing.

Dr. Lucy Hone, the author of *Resilient Grieving: Finding Strength and Embracing Life After a Loss That Changes Everything* explains: "Full emotional expression is an essential part of being resilient. That doesn't mean being falsely positive but rather finding the people, places, and activities that prompt the experience of positive emotions. We know that negative emotions abound in grief; we're looking to balance them out with some of the positive emotions, too." She further explains, "Experiencing positive emotions doesn't merely equate to being happy, but instead includes being curious, humorous, and loving; feeling pride, awe, hope, and gratitude, and the quieter emotions, such as serenity."[xxi]

Experiencing periods of happiness gives you a respite from the hard work of mourning. As you feel joyful moments, let them flow, extend the length, and do not prematurely cut them short. You are activating your life force by allowing yourself to be present in higher vibration, joyful moments.

A young widow, who was a client, had been readjusting to the death of her husband from cancer, and was starting to feel better and look forward to the future. Her fellow widowed friend, however, did not like this progress and judged her for wanting to get better. Instead, my client did what was best for her own healing and welcomed in the waves of joy as much as she could. Although bursts of grief would reoccur, this woman also knew future periods of joyfulness would return and lengthen.

It's far from easy, but you can learn to choose thoughts that bring you healing, rather than suffering. You have the ability to make new choices. With practice, intention, and patience, you can consciously decide to bring in more moments of happiness. Like building a muscle through exercise and repetition, you can develop a joy muscle. Joy is in you, and the feeling can be triggered and found again, even if only for a few minutes a day to begin. As you experience more joy, you will bring more healing to yourself.

Remember, practicing joy is not meant to devalue painful feelings that must be acknowledged and felt. Instead, positive emotions can be experienced and fostered while simultaneously grieving. In fact, joy is essential for your healing, just like all other human emotions.

Use the joy-building practices and exercises below to awaken the opportunities for healing. If these practices don't resonate with you, please visit them at another time.

1. Try this joy-building practice: Discovering Joyful Activities. Think about what gives you pleasure. You may have been disconnected from a sense of joy for so long that it may be tough to think of anything at first. Recall what you liked to do as a child, teenager, or before deep grief entered your life. Perhaps you received enjoyment from the following:

- Watching funny movies
- Reading
- Learning
- Walking or hiking
- Bike riding

- Sitting in the sun
- Spending time in nature
- Swimming
- Gardening
- Playing games
- Watching sports

Grab your grief healing journal and brainstorm a list of activities that you'd enjoy. To start, fill in this sentence, "It's been too long since I_____." If you lack inspiration, refer to the list above for ideas. Add more ideas to your list as you think of them.

Start small and add a few minutes of joyful activity each day. As you begin to feel better, add more time. You'll feel more positive emotions, little by little, when you consciously choose and nurture them.

What activities would you like to try?

2. Try this joy-building practice: Designing a Feel-Good Book. Craft a book with simple things that make you feel hopeful, uplifted, or inspired. Find a pretty journal or a notebook with blank pages. Gather markers, colored pencils, or pens.

Add anything to these pages that makes you feel encouraged or reassured. Write compliments you have received about your attributes, whether it's your generosity, sense of humor, caring spirit, or ethics. Include proud moments or accomplishments.

Paste pictures, write notes, and include anything heartwarming in your book, such as:

- Inspiring poems or enriching quotes
- Cards from your loved one

- Heartfelt notes from friends
- Love notes
- Cartoons

Add readily accessible items to your Feel-Good Book such as favorite photos, greeting cards, or magazine pictures. When you find items that energize you, make it a practice to include them in your collection.

For my Feel-Good Book, I use a spiral artist sketch pad and tape magazine photos of beautiful flowers, home décor, jewelry, and clothes. Because I get joy from beauty, the simple act of looking at these pictures renews me. I keep the book in my living room to browse and add more photos.

Look at your Feel-Good Book when you want to lift your mood. Keep it handy, whether in your private healing sanctuary, by your bed, or beside your favorite chair. You'll activate positive emotions as you leaf through your book.

What else would you like to add to your Feel-Good Book?

3. Try this joy-building practice: Cultivating a Joy List. What are some of your best, most gratifying memories? Record these memories in a list and review it often to change your emotions. Take two minutes now and jot down your favorite memories.

If you have difficulty identifying memories about your loved one that are positive, use memories involving other people. Rest assured, memories about your beloved person will gradually bring more feelings of love than loss as you progress in healing.

Your Joy List may include items like these:

- Remembering the birth of your child
- Learning to swim or drive
- Falling in love
- Attending a party in your honor
- Celebrating a birthday
- Enjoying special times with friends or family
- Graduating from high school or college
- Starting a new, exciting venture
- Landing a job you wanted
- Receiving praise for your favorite accomplishments

After you have compiled your Joy List, visualize one of your memories in detail. Feel the emotions, and remember how you felt. Let the feelings sink into your being slowly, and use all of your senses to recall the memory. What do you see? How do you feel? How do others appear? Notice how your mood is positively changed. You have access to these joyful emotions anytime you want to initiate them, whether in your car, bed, shower, or at work. Since uplifting, fulfilling moments have happened once, they can happen many times again.

For my Joy List, I think about the birth of my son Jacob and relive the elation when seeing him as a beautiful baby. I reminisce about the day my first business opened and feel the thrill again. I recall taking a fun canoe ride on a warm summer night with friends in college. By tapping into the emotions of these blissful moments, my mood improves. When I see, feel, and imagine the memories on my Joy List, I am choosing helpful (rather than harmful) thoughts and embodying positive emotions.

Mark a page in your grief healing journal and label it Joy List for easy access. Review your list and practice reliving your favorite memories often.

What memories could you add to your Joy List?

**4. Try this joy-building practice: Seeing Yourself
Joyful**. To shift your emotions, visualize yourself being happy.
Spend two minutes imagine being elated. This may seem
silly or feel strange, but it works because you change your
physiology. Imagine yourself walking around your house with a
blissful look on your face. You are whistling, humming, smiling,
or doing a little dance. You feel free and peaceful. Observe how
your emotions change when you do this exercise.

Your physical state influences your thoughts and emotions.
Regularly practice seeing yourself joyful, even if it feels
uncomfortable or awkward. Try it when you're doing the
dishes, mowing the lawn, folding laundry, standing in line at
the store, or anytime you are feeling low.

What do you see when you imagine yourself joyful?

By trying or doing different activities, you're gradually
reinvesting in life. These practices take intention and effort.
Like anything new, they'll feel unfamiliar and you'll wonder if
they're worth the effort. Even if you can do these activities only
temporarily to start, they can relieve your mind and body from
the heavy work of grieving. If these joy-building practices do
not resonate with you, skip them or visit them another time.

How can you cultivate more joy in your life?

Learning to Live

"Sometimes I am happy for just one moment. In that one moment I don't think about my problems, I think about all the options I have. I think about all the years ahead of me. I think about all the awesome people I will meet; I think about all the great ideas I will get. I think about all the adventures, about love, about all the places that I am yet to discover. For that one moment I believe I will be happy one day. I know happiness is out there. I have hope."

—Deb Kosmer

As you gently move forward, you'll be able to add more joy, peace, and possibility back into your life. As you feel moments of respite from your pain, you'll be gradually reassessing and rebuilding your life. You'll be cultivating the ability to choose to live in more joy as you mourn.

Your attitudes, insights, and perspectives about life will continue to change due to sudden loss. You'll be awakening more to life's meaning, preciousness, and fragility. You'll become more aware of how you want to spend your remaining time, doing the things you love with the most important people in your life—children, partners, family, friends, and those you care about.

You'll become stronger.

You'll become more confident.

You'll become braver.

You will have gained wisdom from your wounds. You won't be what happened to you, but what you have chosen to become.

Even if you can't believe it now, I know great things are possible for you.

Let's learn to live again, knowing the present moment is all we really have.

Let's shine our light now and live our todays.

Let's live while we're alive—in all our glory, sorrow, challenges, and beauty.

How do you want to live?

Practice Six

Reassure: Provide Peace to Those You Love

Revealing Your Heart

"Say what you want to say when you have the feeling and the chance. My deepest regrets are the things I did not do, the opportunities missed and the things unsaid."

—Jim Keller

When someone dies, many people often have regrets about what they could've or should've said and done when the person was alive. As you examine your life, you may discover you want to express your love and feelings more freely to avoid future regrets. You may know deep down there are words unspoken, things incomplete, and relationships unfinished.

Help your dear ones live better after you die by revealing your heart and sharing what's on your mind now. You'll be easing the uncertainly about the future and preparing your family for the inevitable. You'll be taking away some of possibility of regret for you and those care about when you speak the unspoken, share the truth, and give love.

If you are this far into this book, you may now believe that life does not end after physical death but continues in the spiritual realm. However, those you care about may not have this same belief or know this truth yet. This adds to the burdens of grief. To alleviate some of their suffering, prepare those you care about for loss. By leaving nothing unsaid or undone, you'll be taking away part of the mystery and unknowns often associated with grief from sudden loss. You'll be giving your dear ones reassurance of your lasting love and adoration. You'll be providing peace of mind to both them and yourself.

This chapter will encourage you to open your heart, share your values, and provide reassurance of your lasting love. You'll leave nothing incomplete and provide peace to those you cherish when you follow the practice of reassurance offered in this chapter. Because you've experienced sudden loss, you undeniably understand the time you have left with loved ones is limited. For those you care about deeply—a spouse, child, parent, grandparent, or friend—tell them what's in your heart now. Don't wait.

What would you like your loved ones to know?

Letting Others In

"Every one of us receives and passes on an inheritance. The inheritance may not be an accumulation of earthly possessions or acquired riches, but whether we realize it or not, our choices, words, actions, and values will impact someone and form the heritage we hand down."

—Ben Hardesty

There are undoubtedly still many things you want to say and talk about with those you love. You can give this gift of knowing you, so you and your history won't be a mystery to those who care about you.

By letting others understand the true you and what matters, there won't be unanswered questions left after you die such as, "I wonder if she loved me?" or "I wonder if her life was happy?" or "I wonder why she never told me about her life as a child?" You'll gain peace of mind knowing your dear ones understand what's in your heart, mind, and spirit.

My father died suddenly when I was a young child—only four years old. I have faint memories from a child's perspective. As I grew up, I doubted Dad's affection, wondered if he loved me, and questioned why he was gone. I harbored the false belief that he was not interested in me because he died and left our family behind. When I reached adulthood, I finally realized the painful story I'd been telling myself was not true. Mom would have been appalled if she knew I doubted my father's love, but I didn't tell her or know to ask for support when I was young. Perhaps I was too scared, embarrassed, or ashamed of my thoughts to admit them. Through personal growth work, I began to mend this childhood wound, which was causing unnecessary heartache and suffering.

Receiving a prewritten letter, prerecorded conversation, or loving message from Dad after his sudden death would have been invaluable. It likely could have validated his love for me in order to calm my doubts, uncertainty, and fears. I don't know my father's personality, likes or dislikes, or even if he was left- or right-handed. I don't know what his dreams, hopes, and aspirations were for himself and our family. Most importantly, I don't know what he wished for me, his only child. I would've loved to know any of this information. I don't want others to have this same sense of loss from not knowing the story and life of the people they love.

You can prevent this unnecessary damage by using foresight and a short amount of time now. If you are from a family that is quiet or does not express their feelings and emotions, you may especially feel the void that is created when a person does not make him or herself known. Act now to express your feelings, desires, and wishes to those who will live on after you.

Your history does not have to be a mystery.

Be vulnerable. Reveal your heart. Share your dreams. Make your deepest aspirations known.

You'll live your live with more freedom because you won't have unfinished business and regret.

Choose whatever means is most comfortable to express yourself. You could start a face-to-face conversation, record a talk, make a video, or write a letter. You can give the gift of legacy to those who'll want to know you more. Your children, grandchildren, and future generations will be interested in your wisdom, values, and stories. Share this information now or after your death.

Try this warm-up practice now: Asking Anything. Articulating your authentic self and deepest feelings can be unnerving because you may be doing something new and uncomfortable. Let's try a simple exercise to get started.

Pick a person in your family who died years ago. Choose someone you've heard a lot about, someone you're named after, or someone you are curious about. Maybe you'd love to learn about a grandparent you've never known.

If you could ask this family member anything you wanted, what would it be? Would you want to know how this person met his or her spouse, survived a challenging time, or chose a certain path? In your grief healing journal, note what you'd like to have known or asked. These are the same things your family and future generations will want to know about you.

What will your loved ones want to know about you?

Creating a Legacy Letter

"We all die. The goal isn't to live forever, the goal is to create something that will."

–Chuck Palahniuk

If the prospect of having a face-to-face talk, recording a conversation, or making a video for those you care about seems daunting, let's make it easier by starting with pen and paper.

An ideal way to share what's in your heart is through a simple letter. I like to call this a legacy letter. The advantage of using a letter is that you may find it less challenging to express your feelings in writing rather than verbally. You may feel more safe, open, and comfortable.

A legacy letter is a written record for sharing what matters most to the people who matter most. It's your permanent message of love to ensure your feelings are known even after you are gone. It's your chance to say what you need to say with sincerity.

This concept is inspired from the Jewish tradition of writing an ethical will, which is a written document to pass ethical values, beliefs, and blessings from one generation to the next. It's for anyone who wants to preserve the family ties to future generations. Rabbi Elana Zaiman, author of *The Forever Letter*, explains "The written word preserves the spoken word, and the written word preserves our actions. By writing down what matters to us and by explaining how what matters to us motivates us to the live the way we live, we enable our actions to live on long after we do."[xxii]

You may have experienced the loss of your beloved without knowing his or her thoughts and feelings. You likely would have cherished the priceless gift of knowing his or her words of love.

Think about the last card you received from a parent, grandparent, or friend who died. You may have saved the letter to read his or her words, see the handwriting, and feel the love. This message was perhaps more important than any material possession that could've been received. If you have these cards or letters, find and read them again.

After Mom died unexpectedly right before Christmas, I found a holiday card she planned to give me tucked away in a drawer in her bedroom. It was not yet signed, but the verse said, "May your life be happy in all kinds of ways and may all of your tomorrows be wonderful days."

I believe Mom knew she was near the end of her life but didn't let anyone know, so this was her legacy letter to me. This priceless message was Mom's final blessing for me while she was alive. These significant words make a difference in my life, especially on days that I want to hear her guidance and feel her love.

You can leave such important messages too.

If you feel overwhelmed by the prospect of leaving such a message, start slowly, but begin. There is more risk in waiting than beginning. There is no better time than this moment to start.

Try this warm-up practice now: Saying What Matters Most. Let's make writing a legacy letter easier for you. Grab your grief healing journal and set a timer for three minutes. Label this section of your journal, "My Legacy Letter." Take some deep, slow breaths to soothe yourself. Relax your mind and body. Intend to go deep into your inner self.

Now, gently ask yourself, "What is the one most important message I need to tell my family and dear ones?" Start writing your response immediately. Let all your emotions and feelings flow naturally. Don't censor your response. Continue for three minutes and then stop.

You'll be surprised by the outpouring of love and appreciation you expressed on the written page of your journal. Because you allowed only a few minutes for this exercise, the most important message will be revealed first. You may not even know what's deep in your soul until you begin writing.

Now reflect on your message. Do you wish you'd received similar messages from your beloved? Do you feel a sense of peace for saying what's most important? Would you like to write more?

If you are feeling inspired and in the flow of writing, continue to write. If you like, start a letter to another dear person.

If you are having a tough time with this exercise, I understand. Contemplating your mortality and not being with those you love may trigger an outburst of upsetting emotions. It did for me. I didn't want to consider the possibility of not being with my son, Jacob.

But I did the exercise anyhow. I wrote what I wanted Jacob to know because I knew it would be vital in the future. To get started, I limited my writing to three minutes and just started. This is what I wrote through my blurry eyes and tears to Jacob, who was eleven years old at the time.

Dear Jacob,

I want you to know how much I love you and that you're
the light of my life. When I am not here anymore, I want
you to know I always will be with you from the spiritual
realm. When you can't see or hear me, I will be there. I
want you to know that I always believe in you and know
you can do anything you see, feel, imagine, and desire. The
world is yours to create just as you'd like. Heck, I'll even
be helping you from the other world. Most importantly, I
want you to remember my love. It will be present with you
each day, when you are sad, happy, and even on regular,
boring days. Just call me, and I will come. I'll be by your
side always, and you can always count on me. You are the
light of my life!

Love, Mom.

The message was free-flowing and unedited. This passage is
exactly what I wrote in my first try. It's not eloquent, somewhat
haphazard, and certainly wouldn't win any grammar or writing
awards. That doesn't matter. What matters is the message came
directly from my heart to my son's heart. I told him twice that
he is the light of my life, so that is the truth I needed to voice
from the depths of my soul. He brings so much happiness to my
life. I hadn't fully realized Jacob's impact until I reflected on
my message. This learning exercise provided a valuable lesson;
I recognized the need to prioritize more time with Jacob and
our family.

Most importantly, this simple message of love is now
preserved on paper.

You can do the same. Grab your grief healing journal, the nearest piece of paper, or write in the margins of this book. Start writing now, if you haven't already.

Remember, the benefits to the ones you love will outweigh the pain of writing your legacy message. Your words will be cherished and provide comfort when its needed most.

What do you want to say?

Overcoming Resistance
to Sharing Your Message

> "The only thing you take with you when you're gone is what you leave behind."
>
> —John Allston

Prior to your unexpected loss, you may have thought that "someday" you'd share your sincere feelings or repair troubled relationships. But now you know that in a blink of an eye, your chance can disappear instantly. You have the wisdom that many don't acknowledge—death comes to everyone, including you and those you love.

You may think it's a "nice" idea to write a legacy letter or share your heart's message, but still aren't convinced. You could be apprehensive and have many reasons to put it off.

You may worry you aren't a good writer. It doesn't matter. The recipient will take your love and support over grammar and eloquence any time. You are writing a letter of love and blessing to your beloved people. It comes from deep within your heart, so you naturally have the insight and knowledge to craft your letter.

You may believe you have nothing to say or that no one is interested. That's not true. You are important to many people—your partner, children, parents, friends, and others who love you. Those who care about you want to know how much they mean to you. They want to hear your voice and messages. If your love wasn't valued by someone in the past, this doesn't mean you should stop expressing yourself. Whatever you say will be appreciated by those in your life now. Your gift will be honored and respected.

You may think your family already knows you well. Even if they do, there is more they want to discover and understand. Future generations will want to learn more about your personality, beliefs, and life. They'll want to recognize how past generations shaped and influenced their current family.

Take the opportunity to share your feelings while you can and while you are alive, healthy, and clear-minded.

Try this practice now: Starting Your Legacy Letter. The first step is to identify who should receive your heartfelt messages. In your grief healing journal's section labeled "My Legacy Letter," write the names of the most important people in your life, such as a child, partner, parent, or sibling.

Consider these questions:

- Who would you like to share your feelings with?
- Who do you need to express gratitude to?
- Who can you thank for their support?

The second step is to grab a pen and paper. Keep it simple. Nothing fancy is needed since the goal is to start your letter, not fret over the appearance of your finished work. I guarantee the recipient will love what you write, whether it's on a napkin or the most expensive stationary you can buy. If you feel nervous or didn't already do the first warm-up exercise in this chapter, go back and complete it now. This will get your thoughts and feelings flowing as you get acquainted with writing.

The third step is to start your letter with a salutation. You can begin with:

"Dear _____, I love you."

"My Dearest_____, This is what I want you to know: _____"

"To my family, My hopes and dreams for you are_____."

The fourth step is to begin the body of your message. An easy way to start is to answer this question: "If I were to die today, what would I want to tell my loved one?" In your own words, fill your letter with the essentials of what's important. Include your final thoughts, truths, and values—what truly represents you. For example, if you never told your children you love them, say it now. If you never said you are proud of someone, declare it now. If you never thanked a parent for their love, voice it now.

Remember, your words matter to those you love. They want to hear your voice, know your love, and understand your desires. Your completed legacy message will carry the core wisdom of what matters in life. It will be a testament to both your mortality and immortality—a legacy that will endure for generations.

Your life may end, but your love doesn't. Your legacy letter is a tangible, everlasting gift that can be read over and over to remember you.

What do you need to say to those you love?

Crafting Your Legacy Message

"Put it to them briefly, so they will read it; clearly, so they will appreciate it; picturesquely, so they will remember it; and above all, accurately, so they will be guided by its light."

—Joseph Pulitzer

As you contemplate your legacy message, you may not be sure what to include. Sometimes it can be difficult to find the right way to express your feelings to the people you appreciate the most. The emotions are there, but the words hard to find. To help you put your feelings into words, topics and related prompts are presented in the next exercise to serve as a springboard.

These prompts provide the opportunity for self-examination, which is a powerful tool for improving your relationships and life now. Legacy Letter facilitator Leah Dobkin explains, "The process for creating a legacy letter provides clarity, insight, and a deeper understanding of your life and your family by examining the important events of your life, the choices you made, and your struggles and triumphs."[xxiii]

You may notice life patterns and personal qualities that aren't serving you. As you take inventory of your life, resolve to change anything that is not working. It takes courage to review your life, but if done with compassion and love, you'll learn and grow while integrating loss into your life.

Try this practice now: Crafting the Content of Your Legacy Message. To craft your message, choose prompts and questions from the eleven topics below. Pick those that resonate with you and skip those that don't. Use a few or as many as you like. Be sure to use whatever communication method you prefer, whether paper and pen, video, or face-to-face conversation.

The first group of topics covers your feelings and beliefs about love, future wishes, life, gratitude, forgiveness, wisdom, and legacy. The next group of prompts gives you the opportunity to provide solace to your loved ones about how to handle your death. Topics include remembering you, comforting loved ones, affirming your views on the afterlife, and connecting to the spiritual realm.

Read through the prompts and record your reflections in your grief healing journal. From these written thoughts, decide what you'd like to include in your final legacy message.

Give yourself ample to time to do this exercise. Begin with the first topic below. This is an ideal practice to use during your dedicated time in your healing sanctuary.

1. LOVE: Reveal the love in your heart for those who matter most.

Start your legacy message with love.

Share what you most love about the recipient, such as favorite traits, characteristics, or quirks. Say what you cherish, whether your beloved's smiling face, positive outlook, or can-do attitude. Perhaps you are amazed by your parent's dedication to family, your child's amazing potential, or your friend's loyalty. Express what you have enjoyed about life together, whether getting married, raising a family, going on adventures, or simply appreciating the little things. Tell children how much love they brought to your life.

Your love has the power to heal and transform.

Here are prompts to share your love with the important people in your life:

- I love you because_____.
- What I love about you most is_____.
- Thank you for loving me. The difference you make in my life is_____.

What do you want to tell those you love? How can you express deeper love now?

2. FUTURE: Share your greatest wishes and hopes for those important to you.

Tell others your sincerest desires for them.

Perhaps you want your children to pursue their dreams and marry the loves of their lives. Perhaps you want your partner to find happiness and fulfillment. Perhaps you wish for renewed faith and hope in the world.

Sharing the wishes of your heart to those you love will positively impact their future. Although you won't live forever, your messages can.

Here are prompts to express your future hopes:

- I wish you a life full of _____.
- My greatest desire for you is _____.

- My final thoughts and blessings for you are _____.

What are your future hopes for your family? How can you express them now?

3. LIFE: Share why your life matters.

Explain the significance of your life.

Tell your family what matters to you and why. Perhaps your goal is to be a strong role model for your kids, a supportive and loving partner, or a tireless advocate for meaningful causes. Perhaps you're proud of how you prioritized family above work, committed time to attending your children's events, or dedicated yourself to building a career, serving a cause, or enjoying life's simplicity.

By explaining why your life matters from your perspective, you'll help those grieving assign value to your life after you're gone. Everyone wants to know that the people they love matter.

Here are prompts to express your life's importance:

- I mattered because_____.
- I lived a good life because_____.
- I am most proud of_____.
- My life had meaning because_____.

What matters most? How can you focus on what's important now?

4. GRATITUDE: Express what you are most thankful for in your life.

Tell your family and friends why you appreciate them.

Like many others, you may take for granted the people who are most significant. You may believe others already know how much you love and appreciate them, but it's likely these are the people who need to hear your encouragement the most. Perhaps you want to thank a parent for his or her sacrifices, unwavering love, and tireless support. Perhaps you want to express appreciation to a partner for his or her devotion, understanding, and belief in you. Perhaps you want to acknowledge the things you take for granted.

Your message will uplift and inspire your dear ones now and in the future.

Here are prompts to express your gratitude:

- I am grateful for you because _____.
- I appreciate you because _____.
- Thank you for _____.

Who do you most appreciate in life? How can you express more gratitude now?

5. FORGIVENESS: Offer and ask for forgiveness.

Practice forgiveness.

It's especially difficult to move toward healing if you are carrying bitterness or painful links to the past. Ask others to forgive you. Perhaps you weren't emotional available to family, worked too much, or had addictions that affected others. It's up to you to make amends and ask for forgiveness.

Forgive others. Maybe you need to forgive a parent for not being the role model you wanted, a partner for breaking promises, or a friend for betraying you. It's your choice to hold onto your resentment or offer forgiveness. This does not mean forgetting, but instead, releasing the pain that has kept you stuck.

Forgive yourself. Perhaps you need to forgive yourself because you couldn't stop the person you love from dying. Grievers often believe they should have been able to prevent their loved one's death somehow. You did what you could, knowing what you knew then. Your loved one's death is not your fault. We don't have the power to prevent another person from dying, although we wish we did.

Finding forgiveness in your heart may allow you to find it in others. Offer forgiveness to yourself and others while it's possible.

Here are prompts to express forgiveness:

- I forgive you for _____.
- I hope you forgive me for _____.
- Even though I may not have showed it, I love you because _____.
- Although you may not have expressed it, I know you love me because _____.

What or who do you need to forgive? How can you express forgiveness now?

6. WISDOM: Express your values, lessons, and beliefs.

Talk about what you want others to know.

Share your lessons about family, work, and life. Give the advice you want others to remember. Perhaps you believe it's safe to take risks to achieve your heart's desire and follow your dreams. Perhaps you think you should stand up for your beliefs and be a role model. Perhaps you want to pass down the values and lessons you learned from your parents.

To illustrate, Judith McNaught, author of *Remember When* shares this heartfelt lesson: "There will be a few times in your life when all your instincts will tell you to do something, something that defies logic, upsets your plans, and may seem crazy to others. When that happens, you do it. Listen to your instincts and ignore everything else. Ignore logic, ignore the odds, ignore the complications, and just go for it."[xxiv]

Sharing your wisdom will allow your spirit to reside in others' hearts and minds. You will silently influence their actions now and when you are gone.

Here are prompts to express your wisdom:

- The lessons I learned from life are _____.
- My most important values are _____.
- I strongly believe _____.
- I want future generations to know _____.

What wisdom do you want to impart to your family? How can you share your values and beliefs now?

7. LEGACY: Share what you'd like your life to represent.

With honest, heartfelt words, explain why you lived a good life.

Your existence may have represented service, love, or contribution. Your world may have been filled with family, work, or worship. Your life may have been occupied with trials, lessons, and sacrifice. Perhaps you want to be recalled for your sense of humor, humility, or generosity.

Over time and with healthy grieving, those you love will think more about your life than your death when they understand your legacy and honor your memory.

Here are prompts to express your legacy:

- I would like to be remembered for _____.
- I'd like my legacy to represent _____.
- The words that best describe my life are _____.

What important legacy do you want to leave to your family? How can you influence your life now?

8. REMEMBRANCE: Share how you'd like others to remember you as they mourn.

Express your beliefs, hopes, and attitudes about healing after loss.

Others will long to remember you and will search for ways to do so. When your loved ones are distraught and miss you, share how you hope they can mourn you. Would you would like them to remember the happy times you created together? What fond memories can they recall when they need to laugh? How can they honor your life?

Sharing your perspective on grieving and living before you die will aid the healing process for your family. They will have comfort knowing your thoughts and feelings about dying and coping with loss.

Here are prompts to express how you'd like to be remembered:

- When you think about me, I hope you will _____.
- When you miss me, I want you to _____.
- When you need to laugh, reminisce about _____.
- To pay honor to my life, I hope you live your life by _____.

What do you want to be remembered for? How can you change your life now?

9. COMFORT: Share how you'd like others to console themselves in your absence.

Express how you'd like to be honored, commemorated, or celebrated by your loved ones after you die.

Your wishes will be especially helpful on the anniversary of your death, the first holiday without you, and your first birthday in heaven. Perhaps you'd like your family to eat at your favorite restaurant, bike or walk along a fun trail, watch a much-loved movie, or say a prayer in your memory. Perhaps you'd like them to give a toast in your honor at a family occasion, set a place setting for you at the dinner table, or buy a gift in your honor.

Providing guidance now will help relieve some angst about how to commemorate milestone dates when you aren't alive because your desires are known.

Here are prompts to express your wishes about commemoration:

- On the anniversary of my death, observe it by _____.
- On my first Christmas in heaven, honor my memory by _____.
- On tough milestone dates, remember me by _____.

What can others do to comfort themselves when they miss you? How can you express your thoughts now?

10. HEAVEN: Share and describe your vision of the afterlife.

Explain what you imagine the other side will be like and what your role may be.

When a loved one dies, those left behind often wonder what the next place is like and if the departed is okay. Ease this struggle by disclosing your beliefs now. The questions you want answered about the person you love who died are the same things others will want to know about you.

Perhaps you imagine you'll be greeted by all the family and friends you've ever known. Perhaps you envision you'll be healthy and happy or free and light without the limitations of a physical body. Perhaps you believe you'll guide and watch your treasured ones with loving care.

Affirming your views on the afterlife will relieve some of the fear and questions from loved ones about your existence and well-being after you die.

Here are prompts to express your beliefs about heaven:

- I imagine heaven will be like _____.
- I believe I will be greeted in the spiritual realm by _____.
- I hope the next place has _____.
- My role in the afterlife will be to _____.

What do you think heaven will be like? How can you express your views now?

11. RECONNECTION: Share how you believe you'll stay close in spirit to those you love.

Define what special symbols you'll send to loved ones in the physical world to prove your existence in the spiritual realm.

Tell your dear ones what songs they may hear, what signs they may see, what sensations they may feel, or what knowing they may have. Perhaps you'd like your partner to hear the special song that represents your love story. Perhaps you'd want others to see a butterfly, eagle, dove, rose, or unique symbol. Perhaps you'd want those you care about to sense you through the feelings of peace, love, or comfort. Signs of reconnection can represent anything you choose.

Stating your views on afterlife communication will alleviate some unknowns and take away the longing and waiting for signs. Loved ones can be comforted by spiritual communication when they understand what to expect or hope for.

Here are prompts to express how you'll continue to connect after death:

- I will send you these signs: _____.
- Think of me when you hear these songs: _____.
- You will feel my spirit by _____.
- When you want to feel close to me, I hope you will _____.

What will others experience when they reconnect with you spiritually? How can you provide this vision now?

Sharing Messages for Future Occasions

"Dance like no one is watching. Live like you'll never be hurt.
Sing like no one is listening. Live like it's heaven on earth."

–William Purkey

In addition to writing your legacy letters and sharing your messages for others to have now or after your death, give a series of letters to be opened at future special occasions, such as milestone birthdays, graduations, weddings, and children's birthdays or during difficult times.

Share recollections of special times with the recipient and include heartfelt wishes for the future. Write letters describing how you felt when you graduated, were married, became a parent, or had a significant birthday. Others will know and appreciate your feelings when they go through the same events because you captured your lessons and wisdom. Your relationships will continue after death through these written communications.

After you write your letter, seal the envelope and specify when your letter is to be opened. Look for or craft a special box to hold your letters. Alternately, keep the letter in a family bible, memory box, or hope chest. Your words will be an extraordinary gift when opened during an important time.

What occasions would be fitting for a legacy letter? How can you ensure your messages for these events will be received?

Shining On

"We love them, we miss them, we grieve them. And so, we
live our lives to make them proud."
—Author Unknown

Your time is limited to love and be loved, to forgive and be
forgiven, and to celebrate and be celebrated. No matter what
happens in the future, you'll have influenced your family
and friends with your actions and words. You'll make their
tomorrows happy because of how your messages made them
feel today. In your absence, your written words will mean
everything. In your presence, they will create openness
and communication.

The conversations, written words, messages, and memories
you leave for others will benefit you. You will see yourself
more clearly, understand yourself better, and become more
authentic. Your journey through loss and grief will continue to
challenge you to examine how you are living.

If today were your last day to live, would you be happy with
what you are doing and how you are living? Would your
relationships be full, healthy, and complete? Would you
have mattered?

As you continue to recognize and cherish what's most
important to you, this will be the driving force to make each
day count in memorable, meaningful ways. You'll gain more
courage and stamina to work on your future aspirations and to
follow the longings of your heart. You can live a joyous life—an
existence that reflects your uniqueness and passion—as you
shine on in honor of those you love.

Through the sudden deaths of my parents and my work of helping others cope with sorrow, I have learned about living wholeheartedly and welcoming each day. I have been inspired to live the best life I am capable of living. Although some days I am more successful than others, each day brings a new beginning with hidden possibilities. I hope you will be able to do the same in honor of those you love. I hope you live with nothing unfinished in your heart and appreciate each new day.

Live your life well to make yourself, your family, and your beloved proud.

How can you live on and leave a legacy you're proud of?

Practice Seven

Remember: Honor Your Beloved and Memories Creatively

Memorializing Your Loved One

"Time cannot steal the treasure that we carry in our hearts,
nor ever dim the shining thought our cherished past imparts,
for memories of the one we love still cast a gentle glow to
grace our days and light our paths wherever we may go."

—Author Unknown

Adjusting to the sudden death of the person you love does not mean burying memories, pretending he or she never lived, or getting rid of all personal belongings and tangible reminders. Instead, you adapt to your changed circumstances by using ongoing remembrance, commemoration, and rituals to feel the steadfast love and enduring spirit of your beloved.

Remembrance supports healing through healthy grieving, maintains a continuing bond with your loved one, and allows you to appreciate the legacy of your beloved. Mourning the person's absence invites his or her presence to continue to exist.

Later in this chapter I will give you specific ideas for remembrance, memorialization, and rituals to commemorate your beloved in the years ahead and throughout your life, but first, let's explore the significant benefits of using ongoing remembrance.

First, remembrance is a pathway to healing.

Healing requires remembering. Recollection is a normal, sacred part of grieving. When you define and use this essential practice, it opens your broken heart to healing. Your open heart holds an everlasting, faithful place for your beloved. It's here where you maintain your relationship, not sever it, to provide comfort. It's here where you reminisce about your beloved, not forget, to sustain you. It's here where you continue the bond of love, rather than relinquishing it, to empower you.

Second, remembrance is a permanent corridor to love.

Loving requires remembering. When someone dies, you still love the person who has been an important part of your life. Your love doesn't die. Your grief is an expression of your remarkable love. Recalling your cherished one gives you the means to express this love. Invoking his or her presence in your day-to-day life through recollection allows that love to grow stronger rather than diminish. When you have the courage to remember, rather than forget, you embody love.

Third, remembrance is a passageway to befriending and healing grief.

Grieving requires embracing pain. When you mourn through remembrance activities, you are turning toward your grief, rather than away from it. To mourn and ultimately integrate loss into your life, you need to allow, experience, and express your grief. As you have learned throughout this book, sorrow asks you to say hello to your pain before you can say goodbye; go backward, before you go forward; and descend before you transcend. When you embrace your sorrow through remembrance, you support your natural, organic ability to mourn in order to be touched and changed by the mysterious power of grief.

Lastly, ongoing remembrance is a positive pathway to living.

Living requires remembering. When you find ways to respect and celebrate the person you miss through memorialization, tributes, and personally meaningful approaches, you are making life-sustaining choices. You are affirming your ability to heal and live with greater fulfillment and aliveness. When you are aware of absence, you are aware of life. Remembrance facilitates living.

At times, remembering will hurt and that's part of healing after sudden loss. Your natural inclination may be to run from your sorrow and anything related to your loved one. Don't hide or destroy your memories because it is painful now. You'll revel in your precious memories in the future and throughout your lifetime. The past travels with you and makes you who you are today.

When you use a conscious, healthy process to honor your dear one in daily life, you'll hold onto the love, spirit, and essence of the person. By remembering your beloved in daily life, love continues to exist. As you remember, you'll never forget. And isn't that we all want?

How will ongoing remembrance benefit you?

Choosing How to Remember

"Seeking to forget makes exile all the longer; the secret to redemption lies in remembrance."

—Richard Von Weizsäcker

Recalling the person you miss in meaningful, tangible ways provides a lifeline when you are new to loss, gives comfort as you heal in the years ahead, and allows you to feel love for the rest of your life.

In this chapter, I offer a number of creative ideas and imaginative activities to commemorate the person you miss. As you read through these pages, choose any remembrance idea that appeals to you. In your grief healing journal, note the activities you want to try now or in the future. Choose what feels right or lifts your spirit. Either way, you'll be honoring your loved one.

Whether you repurpose your beloved's personal belongings into a keepsake, participate in a memorial fundraiser, or use a personal mourning ritual, your daily choice to remember is essential to your healing. You will be taking an active role in the process of remembering.

How you decide to pay tribute, mourn, and celebrate a loved one is your decision and yours only. Others may not respect your wishes. Some may share their concerns about your choices. Others may feel uneasy in your need to remember because they are unable to bear witness to your pain. Just let this go because it's your right to remember. It's your responsibility, duty, and privilege to honor the person you will always love and never forget. It's the task of a lifetime.

Revisit this chapter many times as you continue your grief healing practices. Notice how your choices for remembering change as you continue to heal, grow, and evolve over time.

How will you choose to remember?

Keeping Personal Belongings

"Sometimes we are only given a few minutes to be with the one we love and thousands of hours to think of them."

–Author Unknown

One of the hardest questions to wrestle with is what to do with your loved one's possessions: what to keep, what to give to others, and what to donate. Early in your sorrow, you simply may not have the energy to think about this task. That's okay. You can handle this whenever you're ready.

Only you should decide when and how personal belongings are treated. Others may want to "speed up" your healing by advising you to go through belongings sooner or quicker than you would like. This is not helpful and may cause regrets about what wasn't kept. Listen to your intuition to make the right choice to hold onto what is meaningful, special, or comforting. The bottom line is this: don't allow others to decide for you.

Here are some specifics. You may want to leave personal items untouched for months or years. This is perfectly okay. For example, one bereaved mother left her daughter's room as it was for many years after her sudden loss. The mother felt she would've lost more of her daughter by removing items. The mother's choice had no ill effect on her health and did not interfere with her healing. In fact, she was comforted knowing her daughter's belongings were close.

You may want to leave one special item in its normal place. For example, a young woman kept her partner's cowboy boots by the front door where he used to leave them each evening. A client left his partner's favorite shirt hanging in his closet. My stepfather, Wally, kept Mom's purse on the office chair where she used to leave it each day. Even though others may say differently, there is nothing wrong with keeping possessions in their original place. You get to decide how you'd like to be reminded of your beloved.

Alternately, you may want to give some items away because there are likely many people who cared about your loved one, but do not have a tangible memento from his or her life. Items you can part with or which have no sentimental meaning may bring joy to another. Or you may want to add certain items to your healing sanctuary if they provide solace.

Repurposing Personal Belongings

"We can't know why some things happen, but we can know that love and beautiful memories outlast the pain of grief. And we can know that there's a place inside the heart where love lives always, and where nothing beautiful can ever be forgotten."

—Author Unknown

A heartfelt way to remember your beloved is with tangible reminders that come from his or her belongings. There are many inventive, unique options for reusing and repurposing

personal items into treasured keepsakes that you can see and
appreciate every day.

Almost any type of clothing can be repurposed into new,
imaginative items to bring comfort and closeness while
simultaneously give expression to your emotions.

Creative ideas to spark your imagination are below. In your
grief healing journal, note what appeals to you under a new tab
labeled "Personal Belongings" or grab a pen and circle them in
this book. The ideas you capture will then be easily accessible
when you are ready to use them, whether it's weeks, months, or
years from now.

Repurposed Clothing. Pick your beloved's favorite clothes
and transform them into enduring keepsakes. For example, a
widow created a memory blanket from her husband's shirts.
Another griever crafted her deceased husband's ties into a star
patterned quilt to use as a table topper. A bereaved mother
sewed her son's T-shirts into a charming pillow, now kept
on her bed.

Stuffed Toys. Repurpose clothing such as flannel shirts,
sweatshirts, and sweaters into cozy stuffed animals as
remembrances for you or your children. Buttons from shirts
can be fashioned into eyes, and fuzzy sweaters can be patterned
into the body. A widow enlisted volunteers at a local hospice to
transform a few of her husband's favorite shirts into comforting
remembrances. The resulting teddy bears, which were cut and
sewed from the clothes he wore each day, became touchable,
lasting gifts that were loved by his family.

Memory Containers. Use pieces of clothing, handwritten
notes, and greeting cards to decorate a memory box, scrapbook,
or journal cover. Both the inside and outside of the item can be

adorned with sentimental items. You can even embellish the grief healing journal you've been using.

Children's Items. Alter your loved one's favorite clothes into items for children such as hair bands, scarves, and bags. Craft T-shirts into satchels and wool sweaters into cozy mittens and earmuffs.

Paper Weights. Preserve almost any small personal belonging with a simple glass container and a paper weight kit. Choose buttons, vintage jewelry, pins, pendants, watches, thimbles, or distinct mementos for preservation.

Reusable Clothes. Wear the clothing of the person you love who died. One gentleman proudly wears his father's belt, which is now tattered and worn. Another man wears his dad's ties to his job every day. The colorful scarves of one deceased mother have taken on new life for her daughter, who used them as décor at her wedding.

If you'd like to try some of these ideas, but don't have the energy, time, or ability, find an artist, seamstress, or quilter to make a custom item. Look for local artisans or search online. Ask your funeral home or hospice for recommendations.

What ideas appeal to you for reusing your loved one's personal things?

Redesigning Jewelry

"I'm no longer by your side, but there's no need to weep; I've
left sweet recollections I'm hoping you will keep."

—Rita S. Beer, "Just a Memory Away"

In addition to repurposing personal belongings, consider how
you can use a loved one's fine or costume jewelry as a visible
reminder of his or her love. There are many innovative, creative
ways. Here are a few ideas to spark your imagination.

Wear Their Jewelry. Honor your dear one's absence by
keeping reminders of his or her presence close. Wear your
beloved's favorite jewelry, whether a ring, necklace, bracelet,
or cuff links. This is a visible way to symbolize your steadfast
love. If you aren't certain about what to do with your loved
one's wedding ring, wear it on a chain or pass it on to a child.
A young man I know wears his father's watch on special family
gatherings to represent his dad's physical absence. When I
graduated from college, Mom gave me a restyled, modern ring
using the diamond from her wedding ring from Dad. I treasure
this memento of their enduring love for one another.

Design Fine Jewelry. Craft a new piece of fine jewelry with
your loved one's jewelry. Visit an experienced jeweler to get
ideas or attend a restyling event. I reset two pieces of Mom's
fine gold jewelry into new, stunning rings after consulting a
jewelry designer. A widow had the diamonds and gold from
both her and her husband's wedding bands redesigned into
a beautiful turtle-shaped remembrance pin. The first gift she
received from her beloved was a turtle statue, so the pin had
significant romantic meaning.

Create Costume Jewelry. Design meaningful costume jewelry and keepsakes. Fashion a customized necklace, bracelet, or pendant using the person's signature or handwritten message. For example, I had my mother's handwritten message of "I love you," from an old greeting card inscribed by an artist onto a stunning silver pendant. I feel her love whenever I wear this memento.

A young bride repurposed her mother's long strand of pearls into several smaller pieces, including a charming bracelet for her and stunning pearl earrings for each bridesmaid to be worn at her wedding. A bereaved granddaughter, along with her mother and sisters, used her grandmother's costume jewelry to decorate photo frames to give as holiday gifts. Each of these gemstone-adorned frames also included a picture of the grandmother and the recipient from the previous Christmas. The women not only benefitted from this healing activity, but also crafted distinctive remembrances.

What would you like to do with your loved one's jewelry?

Linking to Tangible Items

"Softly the leaves of memory fall. Gently I gather and treasure
them all."

—Author Unknown

In addition to repurposing belongings and jewelry, consider
displaying sentimental items from your beloved. These special
things are commonly referred to as linking objects because
they remind you of your experiences or feelings with your dear
one. Seeing or touching a tangible item allows you to keep the
essence and memories of your loved one connected to you.

Collections. Choose meaningful, distinctive objects that
represent your loved one and group them together in a curated
collection to highlight their importance. Personal items for
a collection might include a keychain, watch, favorite book,
vacation memento, perfume bottle, or pocketknife.

If your loved one was a collector, pick a few of your favorites
from his or her collection and arrange them together.
Collections may include teacups, figurines, coins, books,
seashells, or even Matchbox cars. Alternately, choose one item
from his or her collection and add it to your curated collection,
showcased on a dresser mirror, silver tray, bookshelf, or fillable
glass table lamp.

Draw attention to the objects that matter to you. After my
husband's grandmother Cora died, we chose a beautiful teacup
from her collection. Now, we proudly display this bone china
cup and saucer, adorned with pale pink roses, on a glass shelf
in our kitchen next to a stunning thirty-six-piece collection
of my grandmother Dona's hundred-year-old delicate crystal

glasses. I also display cherished items in a small curio cabinet, including angel mementos to symbolize my two children who died through miscarriage.

Memory Boxes. Group sentimental items you can't part with in a memory box. A young bereaved daughter uses a durable cardboard memory box to keep a collection of significant mementos of her deceased father, including his police badge, photo, and driver's license. She lights up when she shows the treasures from her memory box to others.

A widower crafted three wooden hope chests, one for himself and two for each of his sons. The boys placed these chests by their beds and carefully packed away pictures of their mother, her flannel pajamas, and scrapbook pages she crafted. The widower added wedding photos, his wife's favorite blanket, and childhood pictures. He takes great pride knowing he and his family have precious belongings tucked safely away in beautiful chests.

Mom grouped a collection of small, precious belongings of my father's in her jewelry box, including his keychain; a metal pin that says, "Let's Go Sailing" to symbolize his love of the water; and a miniature metal "K" to represent his first name, Kenneth. I imagine Mom smiling as she looked at these precious keepsakes of Dad's.

Memory Frames. Frame meaningful objects. Anything can be framed. Cards, letters, wedding invitations, marriage licenses, baby announcements, passports, ticket stubs, artwork, or clothing.

A grieving mother glued buttons from her daughter's clothes into a heart shape on fabric and framed it. This piece of "heart" work brings joy to the mother because it reminds her of her daughter's existence. A bereaved granddaughter framed a favorite handwritten recipe from her grandmother along with photos of them cooking together. Now displayed in the granddaughter's kitchen, this wonderful montage is a reminder of her grandmother's influence.

I framed a greeting card from Mom that now hangs in my closet. The card, adorned with a photo of a little girl in a fuzzy bathrobe who is ready to do battle with her closet of overflowing clothes to find just the right outfit, still makes me laugh because it represents my Mom's amusement when I would exclaim, "I have nothing to wear," which I erroneously believed as a teenager.

Framed Photo Home Décor. Gather and frame photos as a way to remember. Collect favorite pictures and choose the perfect photo frames. Dedicate a wall to photos or simply scatter a few framed pictures throughout your house.

Frame a favorite picture of your loved one and give copies to other family members. My husband, Bill, and his brothers received two handsome pictures of their deceased brother, Waldo, from their mother. The remembrance pictures show Waldo doing what he loved, ice fishing. Another couple had a family picture taken the summer before their young daughter died. This priceless picture is now proudly displayed in their living room and serves as a reminder of their daughter's eternal love, innocence, and beauty.

To get started, use sentimental pictures from the photo boards you may have created for your beloved's memorial service. Photo printing services give the option to print your photos onto canvas backgrounds, household items, or custom calendars. Worn pictures or old slides can be restored or turned into digital images. Give future generations a glimpse into their history through preservation of your family's important photos.

Remembrance Books. Create a remembrance photo book. Photo books can be designed to highlight your loved one's entire life or a specific memory, such as a family vacation, wedding, or accomplishment.

If you prefer, photo book services can do the work for you and the results can be stunning. If you're not comfortable with computer technology, recruit a teenager or young adult in your family to create a photo book. Give your recruit the chosen pictures, and he or she can also reap the healing benefits of putting together a remembrance book.

Photo books are wonderful presents for difficult milestone dates, such as holidays, your loved one's birthday, or the anniversary of death. Photo albums are ideal to leave out in the living room or high traffic areas for remembrance and conversation starters.

What important possessions would you like to display, frame, or keep in a memory box?

Using Living Memorials

"A man doesn't plant a tree for himself. He plants it
for posterity."

–Alexander Smith

Remembrance practices can also be taken outdoors by using living plants and trees. Here are uplifting, inspirational ideas to actively mourn your loss while remembering. These healing activities will benefit you now and in the future.

Memorial Trees. Plant a remembrance tree. A tree can be planted in a special place in the yard, memorial garden, cemetery, or at a business. Nothing better represents the cycle of life than a growing tree, from the spring buds to the beautiful summer blooms to the falling leaves and winter rest.

Choose a tree that your loved one liked or pick one with symbolic meaning. Trees represent many healing attributes:

- Oak trees signify strength
- Willow trees represent grief and healing
- Cypress trees denote immorality and mourning
- Yew trees symbolize rebirth and transformation
- Cedar trees represent eternity and protection
- Cherry blossom tress represent fragility and the beauty of life

One of the most thoughtful gifts I received after Mom died was a gift certificate to a local nursery where I purchased a small tree. Now, many years later, every time I look out my kitchen window, I see this magnificent tree which reminds me of my cherished mother. I reflect on how large and strong the tree is which represents the length of my journey without Mom's physical presence.

At Dad's grave, there is a huge tree, now over forty-five years old. I remember watching Mom and her best friend, Lynn, plant this young tree when I was only four years old. Now, this strong maple tree is there for my young son and future generations to appreciate.

Memorial Gardens. Create a remembrance garden, which can be as simple or as elaborate as you like. Whether a few flowers on your porch or a full-blown garden, nurturing living plants is another way to mourn and soothe your heart as you remember now and in the years ahead.

Care for the plants received as memorial gifts, plant your loved one's favorite flowers, choose blossoms that are his or her favorite color, or tend to bushes and plants at the grave site.

Contemplate the symbolic messages of flowers when choosing plants for your memorial garden:

- Forget-Me-Nots signify true love
- Tulips symbolize love
- Bellflowers mean gratitude
- Sunflowers stand for adoration
- Peace Lilies represent peace and healing

I love lilies and use them for remembrance. After one of my two miscarriages, I bought three elegant lilies from a florist to represent my husband, myself, and the baby that died. Although these flowers weren't permanent, the act of purchasing lilies provided comfort. When my cats Emma and Fiver died, I planted a lily for each of them in a memorial garden in my yard, where I also spread a portion of their ashes.

Beautiful stepping-stones that lead to statuary in the garden represent their lives and the love they gave our family.

A bereaved family planted a tulip bulb for each year of their mother's life in her favorite color. Another widow received a huge basket of over five hundred flower bulbs to plant to pay tribute to her husband. Now, her house is surrounded by comforting, joyful flowers each spring. She takes photos of the colorful blooms and shares them with family to remember her husband.

Tribute Messages. Include a tribute message to honor the life of your beloved when planting a tree, creating a memorial garden, or using a lasting monument. A permanent memorial plaque can include your loved one's name, date of birth, relationship to you, a favorite quote, or a fitting saying. Alternately, purchase a stepping-stone with a preprinted memorial message or engrave a favorite quote on a monument.

My husband's family placed a handsome stepping-stone with a touching message where the ashes of my brother-in-law were spread. The message says, "In memory of a life so beautifully lived, a heart so deeply loved." Whenever I visit this site, I find gentle peace from these fitting words.

My father was passionate about his large, successful watercraft business, Ken Olson Marine. Mom chose a fitting epitaph for Dad's gravestone to reflect his love. It says: "Like a ship that has left its mooring and sailed bravely out to sea so someone dear has sailed away in calm serenity." I am comforted whenever I read these carefully chosen words.

What type of remembrance trees, flowers, or tribute messages appeal to you?

Mourning with Symbols

"Sometimes you will never know the true value of a moment until it becomes a memory."

—Author Unknown

Honor the person you love who died and support your healing by wearing a symbol of mourning. In Western society, the practice of actively mourning through symbolic clothing or jewelry has faded. In the past, wearing black clothing or putting a wreath on a home was a symbol of mourning. Today, mourning symbols can be used in new, different ways.

Bracelets and Wrist Bands. Wear a bracelet or wrist band to show connection to a cause, remember the person who died, or show others you're personally affected by an issue, such as breast cancer, suicide, or dementia.

Custom bracelets are often available at funeral homes or online. Add the name of the person who died with a special symbol, saying, or date. When a grandfather of a large family died, the grandkids, ranging from ages eleven to twenty-two, wore white bracelets with the deceased's name and a dove image to honor his life.

Symbols of mourning can open the door of conversation to let others know you are grieving and to build understanding about what is helpful to you. Depending on your comfort level, wrist bands can be worn with the writing on the outside (providing an opportunity to share with others), the writing on the inside (eliminating the opportunity for discussion), or concealed (shielding you from conversation).

Commemorative Personal Ink (Or Tattoos). Use commemorative tattoos to express your internal feelings with an external symbol. Decorative tattoos can range from names, dates, and quotes to portraits and colorful art, such as angels, butterflies, flowers, ribbons, and religious or military symbols. Mixing a small amount of cremated remains into a tattoo is possible, although not all tattoo artists offer this service.

A father whose son died many years ago has a tattooed portrait of his beloved son on his arm with his birth and death dates. He adds design elements to the tattoo each year on the anniversary of his son's death.

Memorial Decals. Display your love through memorial decals. Customized decals come in many colors, sizes, and varieties. Often displayed on car windows, these vinyl decals are also suitable for pressing onto windows in your home, such as a street-facing window or a back-door window. Decals can include the deceased person's name, dates of life, and a loving sentiment. For example, a family who lost their one-year-old daughter designed decals that said, "Our Little Angel, Bella," with her life dates. The design included a bright pink angel because the parent's favorite picture was their little girl in an outfit of the same color.

What type of mourning symbol resonates with you?

Remembering through a Cause for Healing

"Our loss, our wound, is precious to us because it can wake
us up to love, and to loving action."

–Norman Fischer

Support a cause that was dear to your loved one while you pay tribute to his or her life. Perhaps your beloved was affiliated with a church, hospice, or hospital that provided invaluable support to your family. Perhaps you'd like to donate to research for an illness affecting the person who died. Perhaps your dear one enjoyed a favorite hobby, participated in a recreational club, or was involved in an organization you'd like to help.

Memorial Donation Funds. Establish an ongoing memorial fund to benefit the deceased's family or others. Visit your local bank to set up a donation collection or have a trusted friend coordinate the process. Once the fund is set up, you or others can contribute at any time. Online donation sites can also be used. Annual or one-time donations can be made on important milestone dates to your chosen organization.

For example, a ten-year-old boy who was recently killed in a school bus accident had a memorial fund established on his behalf at a local community bank to accept donations to pay for the cost of his funeral. Shawn, a fourteen-year-old boy who was hit by a car, had an online fundraising campaign set up in his honor by his friends years after his death to benefit a children's hospital. The goal of the campaign was to raise $3,300, which symbolizes his football jersey number of 33. The fundraiser coordinator explained, "Thirty years later, we can still feel the immeasurable loss, but we can also still feel the joy in Shawn's brilliant smile. On this anniversary of Shawn's passing, we'd like to share some of his glow by bringing smiles to children and families facing their own unthinkable tragedies." The campaign is running today as I write this, and the organizers surpassed their goal. They are healing while remembering their much-loved friend.

Memorial Events. Sponsor or participate in a commemorative fundraiser. Establish a walk, golf outing, charity auction, or other activity as a fundraiser to benefit an organization of your choice, such as the American Cancer Society, American Heart Association, or Alzheimer's Association. Alternately, funds can be used to set up a memorial scholarship to be given in the name of your dear one.

A family sponsors *Noel's Angel Walk*, the starting event for an annual children's radio-a-thon, which benefits many non-profit children organizations in their community and honors their daughter, Noel. Another family sponsors *Fore Anna's Sake*, an annual golf outing in memory of their beloved baby, Anna. The proceeds are donated to the Ronald McDonald House Charities, which provided a place for the family to stay when Anna was hospitalized. A family whose thirty-year-old son James died sponsors James Fest, which is a golf outing with dinner and music. The funds are used to provide scholarships for continuing education because James was a gifted scholar, earning degrees in both finance and law.

If you don't want to sponsor an event, consider being a participant or volunteer in an activity that is significant to you. If your community has an organized run or walk, join as a family and dedicate your involvement to your deceased loved one. You can design team T-shirts to make others aware of your cause or the important person you are remembering.

Alternately, you can raise funds through selling memorial products such as jewelry, clothing, ornaments, or anything fitting for your cause.

What type of remembrance activity appeals to you?

Using Remembrance Practices

"It is one's duty to love those we do not see."

–Soren Kierkegaard

Use remembrance practices to express your grief and acknowledge the physical absence of your loved one. Use rituals to invoke connection to your beloved's presence in your daily life, maintain your continuing bond of love, and honor your feelings.

Rituals can be simple, such as lighting a candle or burning incense in memory, saying good morning or good night to your beloved, looking at photos, sitting in his or her chair, reciting a prayer before dinner, or spending daily time in your healing sanctuary. Below are specific remembrance practices and rituals to use now or in the future.

Cherished Places. Find and visit magical places to visit in remembrance—such as a park, theater, or restaurant you visited together. Choose a favorite place that brought joy to your beloved or has sentimental meaning. The sights, sounds, and smells can provide comfort, remind you of fond memories, and invoke the presence of your beloved.

I enjoy driving by my childhood home to remember the fun, uncomplicated memories of childhood and the warmth of Mom's love. I imagine us playing in the backyard, cooking in the kitchen, and making crafts. A bereaved daughter, whose deceased father liked to cook, enjoys making food at her father's home using his grill, utensils, and bar supplies. The family makes it a ritual to toast him with his favorite drink at these memorable meals.

Hobbies and Activities. Carve out designated times for remembering a loved one through expressive activity. Resume activities you enjoyed such as a daily walk, weekend bike rides, mountain hikes, or afternoon movies. If your loved one had a favorite hobby, partake in the activity to reignite feelings of closeness.

I loved making chocolate chip cookies with Mom when I was growing up. Now, whenever I bake cookies with our favorite recipe, I am reminded of her. A client whose father died loves going fishing with his son at the same river he visited with his dad. Doing activities from his childhood, he is making new, irreplaceable memories with his son.

Music. Put together a compilation of songs that remind you of your loved one. Include music you enjoyed together, music he or she loved, or songs that make you think about his or her life. Listen to this music in your healing sanctuary or periodically during the day.

My nephew Seth put together a playlist of 1970s music that his father liked and played these songs during his dad's memorial service. Now, Seth can celebrate the music his father loved anytime. When my father-in-law, Norb, died, his children put together a compilation of polka songs to play at his funeral because he was an avid dancer and loved lively polka music.

When we hear this music, our family can see Norb's spirit and imagine him doing what he loved.

Holidays. Create a commemorative ornament, tree, or ritual during the holidays. Make a memorial ornament by filling a glass ball with objects and themed items to represent the person you're remembering. Hang your newly created ornament on the holiday tree or the mantel every year. If you like, involve children in making this decoration to help them remember the person you are commemorating. Over time, you will have an array of beautiful ornaments to signify your loved one.

Display a holiday tree that represents your dear one. This unique tree can be decorated with your loved one's favorite colors, embellishments to denote his or her hobbies and interests, photo ornaments, or anything evocative to symbolize his or her life. Creating your tree is a healing remembrance practice you can do every holiday during an extremely difficult time of year.

Buy yourself a present from the deceased in his or her memory if that feels right. For many years after Mom's death, I purchased presents for myself as symbolic gifts from Mom at the holidays and at other milestone dates. This was another way of mourning and keeping her spirit close.

Give a gift to or in memory of the person you love who died. I donated to many different non-profit organizations in Mom's name as a memorial to her during the holidays. Organizations ranged from hospices to humane societies to children's organizations.

Others in your family may have a different style of mourning. You can choose to tell others about your remembrance activity if that provides comfort or keep it private. Remembrance activities can be a private, yet public way of remembering your beloved, depending on what you choose.

Ceremony. Use ceremony to remember, mourn, and integrate loss into your life. For example, give a set of tea light candles to family members and invite them to join you in a moment of remembrance from where they live, whether for a holiday, birthday, anniversary of loss, or any day you designate. Include an expressive poem or a few carefully chosen words that can be said when the candles are lit. As each person lights their candle, a memory can be shared.

An online search of candlelight memorial service poems will reveal many beautiful readings. Knowing others are paying tribute to your beloved person at the same time will provide loving comfort. A ceremony can become a yearly or more frequent ritual to facilitate healing.

What remembrance practice or ritual would you like to try?

Living While Remembering

"Try to strike that delicate balance between a yesterday
that should be remembered and a tomorrow that must
be created."

—Earl A. Grollman

It's possible you can live not only for yourself, but for the
person you love who died. Your beloved still lives on through
your actions, accomplishments, and how you live your life. As
you heal, those around you will heal too.

Perhaps the gentle relinquishing of sorrow will allow room for
a new, different relationship with the one you miss based on
spirit, love, and memory instead of sadness, grief, and pain.
This will be the space in your soul where the continuing bonds
of love flourish and your beloved moves forward "with" you
in memory and daily life. This is the place where the past and
present coexist as a part of you.

You'll enjoy daily reminders of your dear one's presence,
influence, and love as you remember. You'll be caring for
yourself and honoring your grief as you remember. You'll be
keeping your beloved alive as you remember.

Day by day, you'll continue to move forward just as life
continues to move forward. Notice I use the phrase "moving
forward," rather than "moving on." Moving forward does not
mean leaving the person you love behind. Memories, love, and
influence are always yours to keep. You are moving forward
with the person you love as you continue to live and remember.

You never forget when you remember. When you remember, you heal. When you heal, you live on in honor of the person you love.

How will you live by remembering?

Epilogue

Rejoining Life

"All that I am, or hope to be, I owe to my Angel Mother."

–Abraham Lincoln

Although everyone's grief experience is different, it took over three years before Mom's death did not preoccupy my waking thoughts. I could function with daily activities again, but with a hard-won appreciation of the preciousness of each day and the all-too-personal understanding of life's finite nature. This did not mean that I was over my loss, but instead, I had integrated loss into my life and readjusted to Mom's physical absence. I still had many years of healing to face, but the pain had softened.

Now, many years later, I rarely have sadness, but the things I enjoyed most about Mom are what I miss. I would have loved for her to meet her grandson and see my life now. Although she "knows" in the spiritual realm, her continuing bond of love soothes and dissipates my bittersweet feelings in the physical realm. I recovered from her sudden death, but the sense of physical loss remains. How could it not? The person you love will always be a part of you.

I know an unbreakable bond of caring and connection lives. I continue to feel her and Dad's influence and will for the rest of my life. I can relish the gift of their lives with joy rather than sadness because I choose love over sorrow. There is no end to love. It always will be.

I am healed, and you can heal too.

Surviving Sudden Loss Over Time

"I look back for forgiveness both for myself and others. I look
to the future with appreciation for those that are in my life as
well as those who are not. I look to the future with faith and
optimism that those things that never made sense someday
will, and that great things are yet to happen."

—Anonymous

I am proud of you.

You are a survivor of sudden loss.

Reflect for just a moment on the hours and days after your
loved one died. Look how far you've come. You are surviving
the unthinkable—the death of someone you love and never
expected to die. Anything else will pale in comparison.

You're overcoming what you thought you could not. You are
learning you can live beside sudden loss and heal.

Good days will begin to outnumber bad days. This transition
will occur so gradually that you may not realize healing is
underway. As time goes on, your focus may change from coping
without the physical presence of your beloved to rebuilding and
redefining life.

You do not come through unexpected death and grief
unscathed, but instead will have newfound power and strength
to take almost anything that life throws your way. As a survivor,
you sometimes don't recognize this bravery and capability.

Bit by bit, as you pick up the pieces, you'll be reshaped in a new,
different way. You'll be reevaluating what you want to give and

receive from life. You'll be emerging as a changed person with a new sense of self and identity—one that is formed by who you really are deep inside rather than by what others expect.

You'll be a person with more love in your heart, compassion, understanding, and appreciation for life. You'll be more aligned with your authentic self and true nature as you work toward your reimagined life.

By opening your heart to what you really seek in life, whether deep love, deep joy, deep passion, deep purpose, or deep meaning, you'll create a life you're proud of, a life you love. You'll be cocreating with the spiritual presence and influence of your beloved. You'll be cultivating the power to shape your legacy for coming generations.

Life will return differently, but still beautiful. Still meaningful. Still yours. The death of the person you love will become incorporated into your soul, life history, and identity.

By becoming all that you are capable of, you'll carry your beloved inside your beauty. You can honor the physical death of your loved one by choosing to live fully.

Grieving, healing, and transcending loss will likely be the hardest thing you'll ever do in your life, but the reward will be an existence of meaning, fulfillment, and joy.

You will be strengthened and not defeated by loss. You will be defined by love, not loss.

How will you define your life?

Suggested Reading

Ashley Davis Bush, LICSW, *The Art and Power of Acceptance: Your Guide to Inner Peace* (Sterling Ethos: New York, 2019)

Ashley Davis Prend, ACSW, *Transcending Loss: Understanding the Lifelong Impact of Grief and How to Make It Meaningful* (New York: Berkley Books, 1997)

Lucy Hone, PhD, *Resilient Grieving: Finding Strength and Embracing Life After A Loss That Changes Everything* (New York: The Experiment, 2017)

John W. James, Russell Friedman, *The Grief Recovery Handbook: The Action Program for Moving Beyond Death, Divorce, and Other Losses* (New York: Harper Collins, 1998)

Dennis Klass, Phyllis R. Silverman, and Steven L. Nickman, *Continuing Bonds: New Understandings of Grief* (Washington DC: Taylor & Francis, 1996)

Louis LaGrand, PhD, *Healing Grief, Finding Peace: 101 Ways to Cope with the Death of Your Loved One* (Naperville: Source Books, 2011)

Tom Stone, *Pure Awareness: Five Simple Techniques for Experiencing Your Essential Nature* (Carlsbad: Great Life Technologies, 2007)

Judy Tatelbaum, *You Don't Have to Suffer: A Handbook for Moving Beyond Life's Crises* (New York: Skyhorse Publishing, 2012)

Brian Weiss, MD, *Many Lives, Many Masters: The True Story of a Psychiatrist, His Young Patient, and Past Life Therapy* (New York: Simon & Schuster, 1988)

Martha Whitmore Hickman, *Healing After Loss: Daily Meditations for Working Through Grief* (New York: Harper Collins, 2002)

Alan Wolfelt, PhD, *Understanding Your Grief: Ten Essential Touchstones for Finding Hope and Healing Your Heart* (Fort Collins: Companion Press, 2003)

Elana Zaiman, *The Forever Letter: Writing What We Believe for Those We Love* (Woodbury: Llewellyn, 2017)

Afterword

Navigating grief successfully requires knowledge and understanding of the grief process and a willingness to do the work of mourning. As you begin to recognize and experience most intensely all the reactions to your loss, that is when the real work of mourning begins.

Now that this death has happened, it is up to you to decide what can be done with your grief. In ways that are personal and unique to you alone, you will gradually integrate your loss into the framework of your life as you slowly give up the reality that included the physical presence of your loved one.

The more you learn about grief, the better you can cope with it. When you understand what is happening to you and have some idea of what to expect, you will feel more in control of your grief and will be in a better position to take care of yourself, to find your own way through your loss, and to begin rebuilding your life.

Grief is something that you can learn to work with—you need not sit passively in the face of it, just waiting for time to pass. The worst thing you can do in grief is to try to wait it out or wait for something outside of yourself to happen. The passage of time alone does nothing to heal your wounded soul. Time is neutral. It is what you do with the time that makes the difference.

In grief, we know that certain reactions (physical, emotional, social, spiritual) are common and normal, and most people who've suffered a loss will experience most of them at one time or another. Researchers who've studied grieving people often write about steps, stages, and phases, but these are theoretical models that are meant to help us better understand the process of mourning and to learn who is best helped by what intervention and when.

We now know that everyone grieves differently according to their age, gender, personality, culture, value system, past experience with loss, and available support.

We've learned that when people know what "normal" is, when they know what to expect when they've lost a loved one, they are much better prepared to manage their own reactions and tend to do better with their grief.

We also know that grieving is an active process, not a passive one, and recovery is a choice. Coping with grief involves many courses of action, and learning how to use this grieving time can help you move toward healing and personal growth.

Anticipatory loss begins when a life-threatening illness is diagnosed or a terminal prognosis is given, when we understand that there is no cure, and we realize that death is likely or inevitable. In some ways, anticipatory mourning can be harder than the grief we experience after the death, because when we are waiting for the death to happen, we are on constant alert, living in a state of emergency over an extended period of time.

On the other hand, this period offers the benefit of preparation time, as we and those close to us begin to think about our lives without the one who is dying and how we and our loved one can use the time remaining to reflect, to prepare for the future, and to finish unfinished business.

But when the loss of someone dearly loved is sudden and unexpected, it can feel as if, in an instant, the entire landscape of our life has been destroyed completely—as if someone dropped a nuclear bomb in our midst, and everything familiar, everything we thought we knew for certain, believed in, and took for granted, is now in shambles. It is so unexpected, so unfamiliar, so overwhelming that it can take weeks and months and even years for us to get our bearings, find ourselves once again, and begin rebuilding our lives.

In the aftermath of the death of a loved one, we need emotional support to help alleviate suffering and help to be in the world in new and different ways. To heal through grief, we must also *mourn*—that is, we need to express our grief (thoughts, feelings) *outwardly* and find ways to work through our deep sadness and pain.

But where do you begin? *The Sudden Loss Survival Guide* offers a myriad of useful tools, practical suggestions, and helpful practices that over time can help you move from sorrow to healing, toward a life worth living.

Grief is different for everyone, and what works for one person won't work for everyone. This guide is easy to read and understand, yet comprehensive enough to serve anyone who is struggling with significant loss. It includes not only an overview of what reactions are normal (and therefore to be expected) in grief, but also what can be done to process and deal with them more effectively.

I know of no other book that offers such a vast variety of actions and specific healing practices—truly there is something here for everyone. When we lose someone dearly loved, too often we are left feeling discouraged, hopeless, helpless, and alone, believing there is nothing to be done, and nothing we can do to help ourselves. This guide gives us hope that can we learn not only how to survive sudden loss, but how to transcend it as well.

Grief is a normal yet highly personal response to loss. It is neither an illness nor a pathological condition, but rather a natural process that, *depending on how it is understood and managed*, can lead to healing and personal growth. *The Sudden Loss Survival Guide* helps the reader to do both.

—Marty Tousley, RN, MS, FT

Acknowledgments

This book came into being with the love, support, and light of many wonderful people, both here and in spirit. I would like to give a big thank you to the following people:

Debra Marrs—Your patience, guidance, wisdom, and skilled artistry brought this book into form, and I am forever appreciative.

Jill Swenson—Your knowledge, teaching, and expertise found the perfect home for my work, and I am grateful for your direction.

Maggie Chula—Your divine guidance, connection to the spiritual realm, encouragement, and love was a sustaining force to finish this book project.

Brenda Knight—Your interest, foresight, and knowledge was an extraordinary gift. This book would not be here without you and the Mango team.

Bill Hanson—My husband: a man of integrity, character, and strength. Thank you for your steadfast love, patience, and support to complete this book and always being there for our family.

Jacob Hanson—My amazing son and the light of my life. Keep shining brightly, dreaming big, and following your heart. I'm proud to be your mom.

And to my Mom and Dad—Thank you for your love, light, and partnership to bring this book into the world. All I am is because of you.

About the Author

Chelsea Hanson is a certified grief support specialist and educator, specializing in transforming personal losses into possibilities to embrace life and live with deeper meaning. She is the author of the *Hello from Heaven* series of gift books.

Chelsea transcended unexpected loss over time, losing both her father and mother at a young age. She lives in Wisconsin with her husband and son.

She offers individual grief support counseling for healing after sudden loss.

For more information about Hanson's services, email info@ chelseahanson.com or visit ChelseaHanson.com.

Endnotes

[i] Elisabeth Kübler Ross, *On Death and Dying* (New York: Scribner, 1969)

[ii] Ashley Davis Bush, *Grief Intelligence: A Primer*, The Huffington Post, Blog Post, August 9, 2013

[iii] Helen Fitzgerald, *The Mourning Handbook* (New York: Simon & Schuster, 2013)

[ix] J. William Worden, *Grief Counseling and Grief Therapy* (New York: Springer Publishing Company, 2009)

[v] Ashley Davis Prend, *Transcending Loss: Understanding the Lifelong Impact of Grief and How to Make It Meaningful* (New York: Berkley Books, 1997)

[vi] Dennis Klass, Phyllis R. Silverman, and Steven L. Nickman, *Continuing Bonds: New Understandings of Grief* (Washington, DC: Taylor & Francis, 1996)

[vii] Jim Miller, *100 Healing Messages for your Grief*, video series (self-pub., Willowgreen, 2012)

[viii] Judy Tatelbaum, *You Don't Have to Suffer: A Handbook for Moving Beyond Life's Crises* (New York: Skyhorse Publishing, 2012)

[ix] John W. James, Russell Friedman, *The Grief Recovery Handbook: The Action Program for Moving Beyond Death and Other Losses* (New York: Harper Collins, 1998)

[x] Bradley Nelson, *The Emotion Code: How to Release Your Trapped Emotions for Abundant Health, Love, and Happiness* (New York: St Martin's Essentials, 2019)

[xi] Alexandra Kennedy, *Honoring Grief: Creating a Space to Let Yourself Heal* (Oakland: New Harbinger, 2014)

[xii] Katherine Woodward Thomas, *Calling in "The One": 7 Weeks to Attract the Love of Your Life* (New York: Three Rivers Press, 2004)

[xiii] Sameet Kumar, *Grieving Mindfully: A Compassionate and Spiritual Guide to Coping with Loss* (Oakland: New Harbinger, 2005)

[xiv] Margaret Stroebe and Henk Schut, "The Dual Process Model of Coping with Bereavement: Rationale and Description," *Death Studies.* 23, no. 3 (1999)

[xv] Gwyneth Paltrow, *Vanity Fair*, Issue 552, page 151

[xvi] Louise Hay, *Heart Thoughts: A Treasury of Inner Wisdom* (Carlsbad: Hay House, 2012)

[xvii] Mark Anthony, *Never Letting Go: Heal Grief with Help from the Other Side* (Woodbury: Llewellyn, 2011)

[xviii] Martha Whitmore Hickman, *Healing After Loss: Daily Meditations for Working Through Grief* (New York: Harper Collins, 2002)

[xix] Jim Miller, *100 Healing Messages for your Grief*, video series (self-pub., Willowgreen, 2012)

[xx] Patrick Mathews, Kathleen Mathews, *Everlasting Love: Finding Comfort through Communicating with Your Beloved in Spirit* (Woodbury: Llewellyn, 2014)

xxi Lucy Hone, *Resilient Grieving: Finding Strength and Embracing Life After a Loss That Changes Everything* (New York: The Experiment, 2017)

xxii Elana Zaiman, *The Forever Letter: Writing What We Believe for Those We Love* (Woodbury: Llewellyn, 2017)

xxiii Leah Dobkin, *Surprising Health Benefits Linked to Recalling and Writing Your Story.* www.LegacyLetter.org/ Legacy-Letters

xxiv Judith McNaught, *Remember When* (New York: Pocket Books, 1996)

Mango Publishing, established in 2014, publishes an eclectic list of books by diverse authors—both new and established voices—on topics ranging from business, personal growth, women's empowerment, LGBTQ studies, health, and spirituality to history, popular culture, time management, decluttering, lifestyle, mental wellness, aging, and sustainable living. We were recently named 2019's #1 fastest growing independent publisher by *Publishers Weekly*. Our success is driven by our main goal, which is to publish high quality books that will entertain readers as well as make a positive difference in their lives.

Our readers are our most important resource; we value your input, suggestions, and ideas. We'd love to hear from you—after all, we are publishing books for you!

Please stay in touch with us and follow us at:

Facebook: Mango Publishing
Twitter: @MangoPublishing
Instagram: @MangoPublishing
LinkedIn: Mango Publishing
Pinterest: Mango Publishing

Sign up for our newsletter at www.mangopublishinggroup.com and receive a free book!

Join us on Mango's journey to reinvent publishing, one book at a time.